Don't Be A LAMESAUCE

Don't Be a LAMESAUCE

A Ridiculously Effective Book on Student Leadership

Third Edition

-Youth Mover-

Brandon Lee White

Illustrated by Laura Schaeffer

Contents

This book is dedicated to all youth in schools and clubs who are struggling with tough issues, fighting to find themselves, and wanting to become more.

This is for you.

ACKNOWLEDGMENTS

There are so many people I want to thank who have helped make this book possible:

Jesus–He is the leader and savior of my life.

Rachel White (wife)– You have given me so much to help me become the man I want to be. You help me lighten up and not take myself so seriously. I love you!

Rocky and Joyce White (parents)–You have known me longer than anyone. You have given me support, unconditional love, and guidance. Also, thanks to my big brother, **Ryan White**, who helped shape who I am. Thanks, bro.

Fellow Speakers–You guys have helped by giving me advice, encouragement, and support. Much love and respect for lending a hand or ear when I needed it. Thank you.

Past and Current Clients (Principals, Advisors, and other Decision Makers)–You have helped me expand my speaking through experience and have treated me with awesome hospitality. I know you probably deal with a lot of speakers, but I want you to know how much of an impact you make on youth. Keep up the good work, and thank you!

Youth–YOU are the people this book is mainly for. Thank you for being "awesomesauce" enough to read it. "Let It Move" and live your life!

INTRODUCTION

I'm a work in progress. Everything in this book might as well be written for me, because I need it just like everyone else. It took me a while to realize I was being a "lamesauce." A lamesauce is someone who doesn't become all that they can, because they're not willing to do all that they need to do. And then on top of that they make excuses and blame other people for their own mistakes. They let fear, anger, jealousy, and laziness run their life. I use to be a lamesauce... I was living my life out of fear. I feared not being cool enough. I feared not having a girlfriend. I feared facing the truth. I feared facing myself.

This book is not an attempt to pick on lamesauces and make fun of them, because we would probably be making fun of ourselves. Like bullying, it's realizing that any of us can become negative and do harmful things to ourselves and others. It's realizing that our greatest enemy is ourselves, and if we want to change the world we need to first change ourselves.

So, what is this book about? Well, I've given speeches to thousands of youth around the country on the importance of character-based leadership and how to apply it. This book is a compilation of my past experiences, personal knowledge of leadership, and insight from experts on leadership. This book is about leadership. You don't have to be an adult or the president of the student council to lead, but you do need to be an awesomesauce.

Here's how this book is going to flow. I will start out talking about my dirty dark past, because leaders need to be brave enough to be vulnerable. The core of leadership is being real, because no one will trust you if they don't think you're real. Then we will go on to the "Responsibility Factor" and the "Risk Factor." These two factors "come with the territory" of leadership. We will talk about what leadership is NOT, followed by what leadership is. Finally, in the back of the book you will find case studies to practice your new-found knowledge and skills.

Youth leadership is greatly needed right now in communities, schools, and homes. Sometimes the greatest threat that keeps youth from becoming successful is themselves. Leaving behind our "lamesauce" lives and becoming "awesome" is where we should be, and deep down inside, it's where we want to be.

So, there you have it, this book is a roadmap that will guide you from the road of "Lamesauciness" to the highway of "Awesomesauce."

Youth have so much potential with increasing technology and social networking to make a positive impact. Our country, however, faces serious problems: mounting debt, increasing disparities of income, underperforming public schools, and a concerning collapse in character. In other words, I believe we're becoming broke, dumb, and mean.

I know. I know. Not all of us are, but look at it this way. Our environment influences our thoughts, our thoughts influence our behavior, and our behavior influences our environment. It's a big circle that repeats. If you change part of the circle, though, the rest of the circle changes. Every speech I give has the same purpose: to help people think differently so that they do things differently. In other words, my goal is to inspire youth to take ownership of their life and the doubts that can destroy it.

And what is youth culture like today? You tell me. Is it good? Is it something to be proud of? Who are the role models? Like every generation, there is the good and the bad. So, what shapes youth culture? Well, first, let's look back in the late 1800s when youth culture did not exist. Once the United States entered the Industrial Revolution the standard of living increased as new technologies allowed for more free time and more discretionary spending. With more free time, by working fewer hours, youth were able to go to school. It was at this point these factors joined to create a youth culture where youth could define themselves apart from the adult world.

Secondly, popularity greatly influences youth culture. The music, movie, and fashion industries market to youth, and whatever sticks and is accepted is popular. So, what's popular? Popularity is determined by what is accepted as a whole, which is usually based on humor, sexuality, expression, and the "cool" factor.

Look, I know it's a lot more complicated than that, but this book is not about the history of youth culture or what is or is not popular. Rather, this book is about the potential for youth and the demand for youth to become better leaders. I want youth to think of leadership differently. I want them to think differently about their position in society. Youth aren't meant to just be zombies of fashion and entertainment. Youth are meant to be game changers who can influence people around them in a positive way. Through their fresh insight and connection with pop culture, youth have a unique opportunity to steer this world in a better direction.

It all starts within oneself. It's difficult to lead others if you are not leading yourself. Why? If you are not a role model by "practicing what you preach," others will not follow. If others do not see courage in you, they will not take you seriously when you try to instill courage in them. If others do not see you doing what is right, they will not take you seriously when you expect them to do right. You can't fake true leadership. Why? Leadership is a habit. Lamesauces do not have the courage or knowledge to lead themselves. They're stuck in other habits—bad habits. They let other things such as peer pressure and emotions fling them around like the wind. That's where the danger becomes real.

- We lose our identity because we become what others want us to be.
- We seek pleasure and avoid discomfort regardless of the consequences.
- We react with emotion instead of using our heads.
- We doubt ourselves and give up.
- We become slaves to our addictions and emotions.
- We eventually lose.

Stop.

Remember that the chapters to come are about you, me, and everyone else. They are about us getting real, opening up, and getting fired up to do something with our lives. Maybe that means starting something new, or maybe that means quitting something old. Maybe that means thinking about certain things differently, or maybe that means letting go of certain thoughts that are keeping you back. Maybe that means sucking it up and busting out in a moment of courage, or maybe that means being patient and letting something develop.

Not everyone wants to read "self-help" books, but what is self-help, really? Well, it sounds like it's when you help yourself. Reading a book about helping yourself is a good start, but the book can't do any of it for you. You can know what to do and still not do it. So, self-help can't come from a book, movie, song, teacher, coach, or even a motivational speaker such as myself. Why? Because, self-help must come from yourself. The irony is that you can't do it on your own. We need others to help us. That's why we have parents at home, teachers at school, and role-models throughout. So, self-help starts with allowing yourself to be helped by others, to be taught by others, and then choosing to do it yourself, choosing to help yourself from accepting the help of others.

I am who I am today because of what I chose to do with what others taught me. You can't help others if you don't help yourself, and you can't help yourself without some help from others. Because of some leadership, I now see myself differently. How we see ourselves determines what we make of ourselves. We need more people who are willing to humble themselves and see the "lamesauce inside," open their minds to the help of other leaders so that they can learn to become leaders as well.

Do you want to become more?
Do you want to become a leader?
Do you want to become an awesomesauce?

Well, let me help you help yourself.

"You can't help others if you don't help yourself, and you can't help yourself without some help from others."

- Brandon White

- 17 -

CHAPTER 1

Retired Lamesauce

I'm waiting for my time.

Everything's dark except for the light filtering beneath the stage curtain from the stage lights. I remember past experiences that helped change my life and bring me here. It all seems surreal—almost like a dream.

It's going to be a huge audience.

I remember having these same feelings when I was in elementary school. My classmates and I would be all dressed up in our finest and feeling all kinds of emotions as we were getting ready to perform for a concert or play. You didn't even have to look beyond the curtain. You could just feel the energy, the excitement, and the sheer panic. Mom would be scanning the audience, using the large, old video camera, and Dad would be sitting, arms folded, and asking Mom to help him remember names of the teachers and other parents.

Everyone was nervous or, maybe, it was just me. When I get nervous, I yawn a lot. Yes, I know it's weird. Actually, I'm yawning right now while sitting backstage. But I'm not nervous— not at all (except when trying to remember my speech). I suddenly remind myself, "Attention getter, activity, personal story, joke, activity… Wait! No! Activity, then joke."

My mind starts to drift, wondering how old is this school? It's warm back here, kind of peaceful, actually. I think better in the dark. This reminds me of being in theatre. "STOP! Focus, man!" I don't think I have Attention Deficit Disorder, but that would explain a lot if I did. I can hear the teacher's voice as she talks confidently into the microphone. She will soon be reading my bio, and then I will walk onto the stage to give a speech.

It's funny thinking about how I came to be a youth speaker or "Youth Mover" as I call it. It's been a wild ride getting here while taking several detours along the way…

Don't you hate the question, "What are you going to be when you grow up?" That's the WRONG question or, I guess, less important. The important question is, "WHO ARE YOU GOING TO BE: a lamesauce or an awesomesauce?"

What is a lamesauce, you ask? A lamesauce is someone who doesn't become all that they can, because they're not willing to do all that they need to do. A lamesauce is someone who knows the right thing to do, but doesn't do it because fear, anger, doubt, or laziness. A lamesauce is also someone who isn't true to themselves. They pretend to be something they're not, because they think who they are is not enough.

Maybe you're thinking, "There's no way that I'm a lamesauce!" Don't be so sure. We all have the tendency to slide into the lamesauce role without even knowing it.

Characteristics of a Lamesauce

- Acts one way in front of one person but then totally different in front of another person (in a way that he or she would not want the other person to see).
- Has a cooler life online than offline.
- Does the easy wrong over the hard right.
- Lacks courage and character; won't speak up or go to someone's defense.
- Bullies: cheap laughs, taunts, excludes, harasses, etc.
- Cares more about his or her clothes, image, and popularity than anything else.
- Takes himself or herself too seriously; can't laugh at himself or herself.
- Spreads rumors.
- Falls for any kind of peer pressure because he or she lacks strength on the inside.
- Covers up insecurity by acting like a "jerk" or "super cool kid."
- Won't admit he or she is a lamesauce.
- Gives up when things get hard.
- Blames others instead of taking responsibility.
- Etc.

(I've been guilty in the past of most of the above. What about you?)

Now I'm going to make a personal confession. I was going through some transitions in my life and started realizing what was truly important to me. So, while I was in college I posted a note on Facebook titled, "shed my skin", because I wanted to be open with people about what I realized and who I wanted to start becoming. I started looking at things differently.

Personal Confession

6/26/2008 (1:07 AM)

We often don't know who we are, what we want, and why we do what we do. Yet, we think we do. Some of the things I personally valued actually held very little true worth: popularity, appearance, whom I was dating, etc.

We look for happiness in the wrong places!

Climbing the ladder of artificial approval—"Man, get over it!" That's what I tell myself. We are so busy climbing a ladder that we don't even realize what it is leaning against. Life is not a zip code. It is something much bigger that lies outside of our bubble of pain and pleasure.

*I've "accomplished" a lot so far in my life. BUT FOR WHAT?! Why? Was it to help people? Sure, I wanted to make a positive difference and I still do. However, when I am really honest with myself, I saw a lot of selfishness in myself. I wanted to make a positive difference, but possibly more important, I wanted people to know it. My focus was more on myself than it was on others. I spent most of my time working on an "image" and that's why I don't have many real friends. I spent most of my time trying to build success, and I guess there's nothing wrong with wanting to be successful, but I think I was looking at success the wrong way. I now just have a big lonely pile of "things." **Some people think I'm fake. Some people think I'm a tool... and in a way, they're right.***

A calm feeling sets deep within me because it feels so good seeing it right for the first time (well, more right) but another part of me wilts because I realize just how long it has taken. Do you know what matters? Faith, character, and relationships (modesty, empathy, courage, honesty, confidence, and compassion) are what matter. You won't find anything in artificial appearance, superficial popularity, and other short-term satisfactions. Trust me; I've held hands with them all. I have sampled my own yin and yang: the good, the bad, and the ugly.

We see things when we are willing to look. Mistakes are not the problem; making the same mistakes is!

Take this note as you wish. I'm shedding my skin. I'm cleaning my closet. I'm laying down my defense. <u>We will never be truly happy until we confront what is making us unhappy—whether we know it or not—whether we want to or not.</u>

Man, sometimes we just need to let everything out and clean our slate. Take the weight off our shoulders and confront our fears, shame, and regret.

"I looked in the mirror and saw my worst enemy."
— Winston Churchill

It felt really good writing that note and posting it. I'm not going to lie, though; I didn't want to do it at first. Why would I want to bash myself like that?

Because...
I didn't care anymore.

Or maybe it was because I started caring. Every day we live our lives with masks on, filtering what we say and how we act. These masks try to make us something we're not. Instead of truly changing, we cover it up. It's like painting over something when the old paint needs to be stripped off. It's like spraying on cologne or perfume when you need to take a shower. These masks display us like cheesy infomercials. As you're watching those infomercials you're thinking, "That's stupid. Who would actually buy that? There's no way it is what it says it is. There's no way it can do what it says it can do. It's a fake." That is what everyone else thinks when we live with these phony masks, but in our minds we're like, "BUT WAIT! If you accept me within the next 10 minutes I'LL DOUBLE THE OFFER!"

Funny? Not as funny as you think. Why do we settle for a stupid phony mask that tries to appeal to a watered-down imaginary image of how we are "supposed" to be?

I'll tell you why.

It's the same reason why the small dog barks like a

maniac to the bigger dog that is passing by on the road. Have you ever seen one of these small dogs "go off" for like a 28-minute barking spasm? It's like the small dog has something to prove. Meanwhile, the bigger dog is either totally annoyed or totally amused with the small dog's "mask." The big dog can see through how fake and insecure the small dog is.

We're the same.

Maybe you're trying to be tough.

Maybe you're trying to be hipster.

Maybe you're trying to be a supermodel.

Maybe you're trying to be an "I'm a winner and force a smile" person.

Maybe you're trying to be an "I just don't care about anything" person.

Look, there's nothing wrong with wanting to be more hipster, more attractive, or more successful. The problem is balance and priority. It's like that person who buys a clock at a garage sale, because it's a collector's item and "trendy". After hanging it up, a friend stops by to visit and says, "Cool clock, Jim." Suddenly, Jim is not "Jim" anymore. He is "COOL CLOCK JIM". So he goes out and buys hundreds of clocks and hangs them on every inch of space in the house. He even starts stealing clocks from his relatives, because the more clocks he has the cooler Jim will become. Finally, after non-stop clock shopping and stealing, Jim invites his friend back over. His friend walks in, looks around, turns to Jim and says, "Dude, what the heck is wrong with you? Why do you have so many clocks? Why do you care that much about clocks? Why have you been spending all your time thinking about clocks? YOU ONLY NEED ONE OR TWO CLOCKS!" Jim used to be "Cool Clock Jim", but then he got his balance and priorities messed up. Now he's "Crazy Clock Jim". You see, Jim needs to focus on being the best Jim he can be, but he doesn't need a clock to do that. Clocks are fine, but he thought that "one thing" would make up for what he lacked inside... poor Jim.

Listen, straight honesty coming at you right now: Focus on being legit on the inside, and it will show on the outside. There is a person you are on the inside before all the other crap covers it up. You need to work on that person and stop "bedazzling" your mask. Don't wear a mask, and don't be a "Crazy Clock Jim".

Let me explain a little more about where I came from and why I decided to change.

Wearing a Mask

I was student body president, homecoming king, varsity sports captain, and a drum major. I was also in theatre, SADD, Choir, forensics, debate, and NHS. In many ways, I was the "All-American Boy." Huh. Who was I fooling?

On weekends I wore a different mask. I threw parties at my parents' house and did—well, let's just say there's not much I didn't do. I wanted to be cool. I wanted to drink. I wanted to date hot girls. I wanted to have fun. And it was fun, but fun is not always true happiness.

I realized that I was NOT being completely true to what I believed in. I was willing to bend my morals in order to gain acceptance. You know, not everyone in school drinks, or smokes pot, or sneaks outs. Some students did not care if I did those things. They would have liked me for me. So, why did I care about gaining the approval of the other students?

I'm not sure.

I think whether we want it to be true or not, the culture of "cool" includes those things I listed. I'm not saying it should, but I think the peer pressure is there nevertheless. You can say no and stick with your morals, but you have to be willing to take some heat for it. I guess that's how we know how strong our convictions really are.

Listen, although I had it all, I was very empty inside, because I was being fake to a lot of people, including myself. It's like a race. Everyone seems to be chasing something. Usually, it's something like appearance, popularity, acceptance, or love. Think of it as a job interview. Most people go into a job interview putting their best foot forward. They want to say all the perfect things and look the perfect way in hopes of not being rejected.

Why don't we just be ourselves? Because, we think our "self" is not good enough. Insecurity brings on feelings such as self-doubt and anxiety. To reverse these uncomfortable feelings, we look for fixes. We want easy happiness. We want to have fun, and we want people to like us. We're willing to exchange integrity for comfort. We will mimic others by talking the way they talk, acting the way they act, dressing the way they dress, saying what they say, doing what they do, and sharing their same ideas and values in hopes of being happy, popular, or liked the same as the others seem to be. The question is: Are they also feeling insecure and doing the same as we are doing?

Watch certain reality shows and suddenly you have a literal example. Visualize the drama scene of a girl trying to be a certain something, trying to get a certain someone, and trying to look a certain way for that certain someone to help her become that certain something.

When we base our happiness on superficial things, we will never find true happiness. Why? Because you always have to chase those things. You never have control over those things. In other words, your happiness is determined by other things and other people.

I cared way too much about stupid things that should have gotten me into big trouble. I was lucky that didn't happen. I remember a defining moment when I stood up to my "lamesauce" life and punched it right in its ugly face...

"You cannot be who you are and who you are not at the same time."

– Brandon White

Choosing Your Friends

I was in college and I started learning ballroom dances like swing and salsa. I taught at a dance studio and that studio had dance parties every Saturday for youth. Teens could come to the studio to learn these dances and dance from 7 p.m. to around 1 a.m. the next morning. I loved it because the dancing was fun and because I met a bunch of cool, new people around the same age as myself. What's weird, though, was I realized I was having more fun swing dancing than doing the whole "drinking and partying thing." I couldn't really figure it out. I mean, the "drinking and partying" thing is what everyone did, right? And it was fun, right? Well, the truth is that it's kind of fun as long as you don't get caught, get a DUI, end up in a car accident, overdose, and on and on. And, yeah, a bunch of people do it. But as I watched these people swing dance I could see that they had what all the other party people didn't have—peace. The people at the studio didn't care so much about all the stupid things party kids care about. They were real.

One weekend I was at the studio and the night had just started. Everything was good as usual. I was dancing and hanging out with new friends when all of a sudden I got a text from an old friend from my old lifestyle about a party. Without knowing it, I stood at a crossroads. Do I stay here or do I go to the party?

I went to the party.

It was like I took off the new hat I was wearing and put back on the old hat of partying. I realized I was living two lives at that point, and I was torn. I mean, I still kind of liked my old friends and their partying ways, but I also liked my new friends at the dance studio.

I was confused.

After the party was over, I was driving home, and it hit me. I was not happy.

I was not happy being a fake and doing things just because "that's what I used to do." I was tired of chasing an image of being cool. I was tired of feeling as though I was going to miss out on "something" if I didn't go to the party. WHAT'S THAT "SOMETHING"! Being honest with myself, I had more fun at the *dance studio than out there partying. Why? My friends at the studio were real—that's why. They were not like the others who would stop liking me or would get upset with me if I didn't drink with them. Most importantly, though, it was because I was happy being myself around my dance studio friends. Why did I feel like I couldn't be myself around my partying friends? As I thought about it, maybe it was because they were not really my friends. It was at that moment I shoved the truth into my "lamesauce" mouth and swallowed hard.*

It's scary changing when you've known something familiar for so long and when you have people who will judge you for changing. At the same time, there are others who will congratulate you for changing and will say, "Welcome back." I think we all start our lives genuine and real. We all start as a young "awesomesauce." But somewhere along the way, fear, insecurity, jealousy, negative influences, and other things make us something we're not—something bent on an image of popularity, something that seems right, yet, is completely wrong. We become a "lamesauce." It took me a while to figure this out. Finally, after seeing that the way I was living really wasn't making me happy, I made that radical decision.

I <u>stopped</u> constantly trying to impress people.
I <u>started</u> hanging out with friends who cared about me.
I <u>started</u> looking at myself without a mirror.
Something weird started to happen—something I never really remember feeling before—I felt, well, good.

Focus on being a better friend. That's a much better feeling than trying to make everyone like you. Plus, the weird thing is when you do the first part, the second part usually follows. This is what you have to do if you want to feel secure and live on solid ground. Super Leaders seek to be real and to do what is right and that will ultimately lead to being liked and respected for the right reasons.

Solid ground is peace of mind through not trying to be perfect, but instead trying to work on balance and priorities. Solid ground is knowing who you are even if it's not who you ultimately want to be. Solid ground is focusing on virtues/faith and basing your decisions on those virtues: honesty, respect, responsibility, and loyalty. Solid ground allows us to be at peace even when the world is moving because we're not constantly trying to change, like a chameleon to the color of the week. Solid ground is living for something greater than you. Solid ground is WAY more valuable to a person than gold, but the problem is that most people don't understand solid ground or are distracted by the shimmery short-term things in life.

"You can make more friends in two months by becoming interested in other people than you can in two years by trying to get other people interested in you."

-Dale Carnegie (*How to Win Friends and Influence People*)

KEY POINTS:

- We are lamesauces whenever we do the easy wrong over the hard right by being fake, manipulative, and self-centered.

- We all have a natural tendency to become a lamesauce, because it's easier than having the courage to become an awesomesauce.

- We will never be truly happy until we confront what is making us unhappy—whether we know it or not—whether we want to or not.

- Stop "bedazzling" your mask.

- Solid ground is knowing who you are and allowing yourself to be that.

CHAPTER 2

The Responsibility Factor

The curtains are black. "Why would they make them black? It's hard enough finding the center opening to make my way out." Green. They should make them green. I let out another big yawn.

I speak at school assemblies and youth conferences such as 4-H, FFA, DECA, FCCLA, STUCO, BPA, FBLA, GEAR UP, and others. Some people say, "Wow, you're really blessed to be a natural speaker." Bahahaha! I was NOT born a natural speaker

Shy Kid with a Speech Impediment

A kid was sitting alone in preschool. None of the other kids would talk to or play with him. Although the boy was shy, he had tried to talk to the other kids, but for some reason, they just ignored him. So, the boy just sat there by himself and wondered why no one liked him.

One day when the parents arrived at the preschool to pick him up, the teacher told them, "Your son has a speech impediment, and the other students can't understand him. It would be best if you removed him from preschool and put him in speech therapy." His mother was worried. What would this do to her son's self-esteem? How would he transition back into school?

His dad, however, was positive and knew his son would be okay. When the boy wasn't in speech class, he created

imaginary worlds in his head and acted them out. His mom watched him as he talked out loud, acting out scenes when he thought no one was around. The boy also drew superheroes with his older brother, who seemed to be the only person able to understand what he was saying.

At times, the boy got so frustrated and mad for not being able to talk normal that he spoke gibberish on purpose—and then stop talking altogether. He was mad that he wasn't normal and wished he had some friends. He thought, "Why me?" But he finally realized that being mad didn't make him feel any better. He knew the other kids were mean for not playing with him, so he decided that he would never be like them. The boy eventually grew out of his speech impediment, just like his dad had predicted, and went on to become a national youth speaker at schools and youth conventions all over the country.

That shy kid with a speech impediment was me.

When I was young, I couldn't speak. Now, my job is to speak. Cool, huh?

You can look at your circumstance and say, "If only I hadn't been born poor," "If only I hadn't been born with this disability," "If only this unfortunate thing hadn't happened to me," or "If only I had his (or her) looks." "If only ...."

"If only" is a big, fat lie!

Your worst enemy and biggest obstacle in life isn't a lack of money, a disability, or physical looks. There are a lot of happy and successful people who are poor, have a disability, and don't look like a supermodel. More importantly, though, there are many, many more sad people who think life is unfair and meaningless, yet they are rich, healthy, and good looking. How sad.

Your worst enemy and biggest obstacle in life is not drugs, negative peer pressure, or bullying. It's something way more dangerous. It's you.

Why do I say this?

- Because <u>you</u> are the person who ultimately says, "Yes" or "No."
- Because <u>you</u> are the person who ultimately decides to do it or not to do it.
- Because <u>you</u> are the person who ultimately makes excuses or takes responsibility.

Don't let fear, insecurities, or anything else keep you from being you. If you are weak within, you will fall for anything. But if you are strong within, you can <u>fight</u> for anything.

UNLIKELY SUCCESS:

Despite the Odds

A poor teenage mother in Mississippi gave birth to a daughter on January 29, 1954. Because the mother was so poor, she had trouble providing her baby with shoes. They lived in a house with no flushing toilets. The little girl's childhood was plagued with sadness. At nine, she was raped, and at fourteen she gave birth to a son who died in infancy. She pressed on, and at nineteen, while still in high school, she landed a job co-anchoring the evening news at her local radio station. From there, she worked her way up to having her own talk show and becoming the first black woman billionaire. Her name is Oprah Winfrey.

Don't Wait on Success; Work on Success

In 1978, a young man was living in a camper van with his family in Canada. He worked eight-hour shifts at a tire factory. His passion was comedy, so he took a big risk and moved to Los Angeles to be a comic. He got a break and started appearing at The Comedy Store in the early '80s as Roger Dangerfield's opening act. Later, he made friends with the Wayans brothers and got a gig on the show In Living Color. Today, Jim Carrey is considered one of the funniest and most successful actors of all time.

Opportunities Come to Those Who Prepare for Them

On March 1, 1994, an eighteen-year-old girl gave birth to a son. As a single mother, she worked several low-paying office jobs to make ends meet. As the boy grew, he taught himself to play the piano, drums, guitar, and trumpet. In early 2007, when he was twelve, he sang a pop song for a local singing competition and placed second. His mother posted a video of her son's performance on YouTube for family and friends to see. As she continued to upload videos, her son's popularity grew with the public. In 2008, thirteen-year-old Justin Bieber was signed to Raymond Braun Media Group (RBMG), a joint venture between Braun and Usher. He now has toy dolls of himself.

Fact: Someone will always have it better than you, *and* someone will always have it worse than you. It's easy to make excuses. Oprah had a lot of excuses. I had a lot of excuses. I mean, I had a speech impediment, and now I am a professional speaker!

You have a lot of excuses. It's easy to make excuses. It's hard to take responsibility. If you chase after other people's possessions looking for greener pastures, you'll only end up depressed and discouraged. It's like a dog chasing its tail. Even if you do get that thing you always wanted, you'll find something else that you don't have.

"It is easier to be better than somebody else than to be the best we can."

- Anonymous

Happiness is not having the best of things; it's making the best of things.

—Anonymous

If you think your life is unfair for whatever reason (bad parents, bad luck, fill in the blank), you might be right. There are a lot of people who are in undesirable situations, but here is the reason why people end up miserable in life. Bad situations happen, but if you only focus on you, you, you (what you have that you don't want or what you don't have that you want), then you will always be thinking in a negative perspective. Just like the quote above says, "Happiness is not having the best of things, it's making the best of things." Furthermore, material things are never a long-term solution to making us happy. That's why you see some people miserable even when they have everything. When we focus on helping others, we begin to lose the selfish sorrow that comes from trying to be our own king or queen. When we are humble, we are more grateful. Don't think less of yourself, think of yourself less. Think more of others, and you will start thinking like a leader.

Success is not dependent upon positions or conditions. Success is dependent upon choices. Making excuses is easy. Choosing to take responsibility is hard. Leading is about taking responsibility, and it's also about holding others accountable for their responsibilities.

It is impossible to feel grateful and depressed in the same moment.
—Naomi Williams (Author)

Think of superheroes. What's the difference between superheroes and supervillains? Both have something traumatic happen to them, but the difference is how they respond to that trauma. AND, what leaders they have in their life to help them respond to that trauma and then become a leader themselves.

SUPERMAN vs. LEX LUTHOR

Superman was an orphan sent to Earth because his home planet was blown up, but he vowed to a life of service and justice. Superman's villain, Lex Luthor, was abused as a child and grew up in poverty. Luthor vowed to be a "self-made" man bent on power. The difference: Superman had the leadership of his adoptive parents.

BATMAN vs. BANE

Batman's parents were killed by criminals, so Batman vowed to live a life of service and justice. Batman's villain, Bane (according to *Dark Knight Rises*), was born in a prison without his parents. Bane turned to anger and revenge. The difference: Batman had the leadership of his butler, Alfred.

SPIDER-MAN vs. DR. OCTOPUS

Spider-Man's uncle was killed by a burglar, and even though Spider-Man felt like it was his fault he still vowed to a life of service and justice. Spider-Man's villain, Dr. Octopus, was abused by his father growing up and bullied in school. Dr. Octopus turned to anger and revenge. The difference: Spider-Man had the leadership of Aunt May.

The list goes on. We are no different than those superheroes and supervillains. Bad things happen to us, and we either turn it toward good or we turn it toward bad. It's often the leaders in our lives that help us make that decision. But, they can't make the decision for us. There are examples of people who had leaders, but still chose the dark side. Darth Vader, for example, started as the boy Anakin Skywalker. Anakin had painful events from the past, but he also had the leadership of Obi-Wan Kenobi. Despite that leadership, Anakin chose the dark side because of his anger and increasing power gained through Obi-Wan's leadership.

Listen, there are things that happened and it doesn't matter why or what. What matters now is who you want to be–a superhero or a supervillain–an awesomesauce or a lamesauce? To become an awesomesauce starts with courage and humility, the courage and humility to seek help from leaders, and the courage and humility to become better without becoming prideful.

It's like sailing. Sailors can't control the winds, but they can control how they adjust their sails. If you focus on things you can't control (the wind), you will never get what you want, and you will always be unhappy. If you focus on what you can control (adjusting the sails), you can accomplish your goals and become happy.

Sometimes you can't choose what happens to you, but you can always choose how you respond to what happens. And that will affect what happens to you next!

Taking RESPONSIBILITY

Responsibility is an obligation to respond, because of your ability and the value of doing so.

> Whether you own a car or drive your parents' car, you have a responsibility to take care of it. Why? Because, it has value, and you are able to respond to protecting that value. If you're not able to take care of it you shouldn't drive it, because that would be irresponsible.

So, you might say, "Yeah, well it's my car, and I should be able to crash it whenever I want, Mr. Speaker Man!" Okay, that's fine, but you're not a responsible person. You can do what you want and make your own decisions, but that doesn't mean they are good decisions. A responsible person creates more value by growing what he or she has been given. An irresponsible person devalues by neglecting what he or she has been given. A responsible person toughens up and has a positive attitude, even when it gets unpleasant. An irresponsible person whines like a baby and is quick to give up or make excuses.

Awesomesauce = Responsible Person
Lamesauce = Irresponsible Person

Entrepreneurship

Throughout my life I started and managed several businesses. Below are two short stories about two specific businesses I developed and that, ultimately, developed me:

Brandon's Lawn Care

When I was a freshman in high school, my first job was mowing lawns in and around my neighborhood. My brother or mom would drive me around to all the houses, and I would run up to each house and slip a fancy Word Art flier in the door titled, "Brandon's Lawn Care." Oh yeah, I thought I was big stuff. With the lawn mower, weed eater, and leaf blower filled up with gas, I eagerly awaited my first customer. There's a sense of pride that comes with "doing your own thing." When you take responsibility and ownership for something, you will work harder to maintain it.

Within a couple of days my list of clients grew to four. WOOHOO! That's okay, though, because I would load up my equipment in my Dad's truck and he would drop me off at my jobsites. Other times, I would carry the weed eater in one hand and the leaf blower in the other hand and use my stomach to push the lawn mower down the street to each house.

Brandon's Lawn Care flourished over the next three years, maintaining, at times, six clients! Yes, I know—big bucks. During my senior year, I collaborated with two of my friends, and together we worked as a team. We ended up managing about twelve yards and split the money evenly.

Brandon's Lawn Care was my first taste of responsibility with the possession of my equipment and my position as owner. It was also my first experience in entrepreneurship, and it wouldn't be my last.

Happy Rhino Clothing

While in college I was in theatre and met a friend who would eventually change the course of my life. His name was Jaqwan, and he was a very talented person. Jaqwan was an amazing artist, hip hop dancer, illustrator, actor, musician, designer, and much more. Quickly we hit it off and became friends. We discovered that we had many of the same interests in entrepreneurship. At the time I was doing a lot of acting and modeling and getting my degree in Business Management. Meanwhile he was sketching designs for clothing. BINGO! We decided to put our skills and passions together and start an activist clothing line. One problem, though. We had never done this.

I mean, there's a lot that goes into starting a business, and I'm not talking about a high school lawn cutting business. I'm talking about a real legal business! What was it going to be called? What was the style going to be? To whom were we going to market? How much would it cost? How do we do all the legal paperwork? How do we make the website? How do we fund it? Who produces the materials? And on and on AND ON!

Sometime in February 2006 Jaqwan and I were sitting in my dorm room with a lot of excitement and anxiety. I grabbed a mini basketball off the bed, "Okay, we'll use the ball to help decide who gets to talk and we'll brainstorm everything out." For about an hour we tossed the ball back and forth throwing out ideas. Quickly we realized that there were details we didn't agree on. How were we to decide what to do—flip a coin? It's hard finding that "win-win" solution as they say, and I could see how this friendship might break under the mounting responsibility.

We decided to name our new company "Happy Rhino." TA-DAH! Wait, what the heck does Happy Rhino mean? Well, it means to have "thick skin like a rhinoceros" and to stick up for what you believe in. It was clothing for a cause. Over the next three years, while in college, we created a website, produced casual clothing, put on fashion shows, appeared in local media, raised money for multiple charities, and learned a lot about owning a business. I did a lot of growing up during those years. Actually, I believe I sacrificed a lot of the "college experience" in *order to own a business. Countless hours were spent in the computer lab working on the never-ending tasks. Jaqwan and I, at times, got into huge arguments over, well, just about everything. We would scream at each other and call each other names, but looking back, we both agree that creating and running this business revealed us and made us.*

Jaqwan and I are still good friends to this day, and Happy Rhino was an experience we couldn't learn in a textbook. The thing I learned about responsibility is that sometimes you choose it and other times it chooses you. But either way, it's a test. Like any test, it takes preparation, adaptation, endurance, and a perspective that what you do or don't do affects you, the people around you, and what will happen tomorrow. We can run from it, we can give up on it, but the best way to handle responsibility is to grab it and form our decisions as they form us. Responsibility reveals us and then makes us. How will you respond?

Take on something you are passionate about. Trust me, nothing beats "hands-on" experience, and it doesn't matter how old you are. What matters is how brave you are, how determined you are, and how responsible you are. The best thing about responsibility is that we decide what we do with it.

Have you seen the Rocky Balboa movie? You remember those boxing movies? Well, in this particular one, he's older and now giving his son advice. Rocky is telling him to take responsibility and lead his life. Every time I hear this part I get totally pumped up and consider running into the street with an over-sized medieval sword.

"But somewhere along the line, you changed. You stopped being you. You let people stick a finger in your face and tell you you're no good. And when things got hard, you started looking for something to blame, like a big shadow.

Let me tell you something you already know. The world ain't all sunshine and rainbows. It's a very mean and nasty place and I don't care how tough you are; it will beat you to your knees and keep you there permanently if you let it.

You, me, or nobody is gonna hit as hard as life. But it ain't about how hard ya hit. It's about how hard you can get hit and keep moving forward. How much you can take and keep moving forward. That's how wining is done!

Now, if you know what you're worth then go out and get what you're worth. But ya gotta be willing to take the hits, and not pointing fingers saying you ain't where you wanna be because of him, or her, or nobody! Cowards do that and that ain't you! You're better than that!"

-Rocky Balboa

Tough it up and take action by taking responsibility instead of giving up by making excuses. Courage is doing the right thing even when you don't feel like it, when you're scared, or when it's unpopular. Being responsible takes courage and humility, and that's what a leader does.

Grade Yourself

What if you could grade your own papers in school? Yeah, right, that will never happen! Well, I'm going to give you the opportunity and challenge to grade yourself. The only catch is that you have to be honest. Don't be too strict, and don't be too easy. This is not for me or anyone else; it is for you. Sometimes we don't stop to think how <u>we</u> are doing in "life."

Your challenge is to grade yourself based on how well you have done with "accepting and handling responsibility" in different areas of your life, throughout your entire life. Don't skip this part. Do it. Writing it down is important because it increases awareness. You can write it in this book or on a separate piece of paper. The purpose is not to make you feel good or bad but to help you consciously critique yourself. 1 is worst and 5 is best... FYI.

Responsibility
    1 (Come on, really?) 2 (Embarrassing) 3 (Just Average)
    4 (Good) 5 (Not Trying to Brag, But...)

      School (homework, clubs, etc.): _____
      Friends (being there, honesty, etc.): _____
      Family (parents and siblings): _____

(Total your scores and see how you graded yourself by comparing your total number to the following chart.)
    1-5 = C
    6-10 = B
    11-15 = A

No matter what your grade, the purpose is awareness and improvement. If you received an A, your goal is to maintain the A and set the standards higher. If you received a B or a C, you have some work to do. Keep reading.

KEY POINTS:

- Your biggest enemy is yourself, because no matter what you're born with or what someone does to you, you still make the final decision of what to do about it.

- Happiness is not having the best of things; it's making the best of things.

- It's easy to make excuses. It's hard to take responsibility.

- The difference between superheroes and supervillains is how they respond to traumatic events and who leads them through it. We need leaders to become leaders.

- Being responsible is responding to an obligation because of your ability to do so and the value of doing so (value not just for you, but for others).

CHAPTER 3

The Risk Factor

My microphone is wireless and hands-free. I hook it on my hip and snap the lapel on my tie. Don't you hate it when people do sound checks on microphones? "CHECK, CHECK, Ch--ch--CHECK! Chickidy-Check! HELLO, hey, HEY, HEEEEY... yup, sounds good." I mean, what do you say while testing a microphone without sounding like a complete idiot? I don't know either, but I'm working on it...

I think it's funny when I speak at an FFA or 4-H conference and tell people that I grew up on a farm. Their response is always one of surprise as they tell me that they never would have guessed just by looking at me. Well, let me just say, "You can take the boy out of the country but YOU CAN'T TAKE THE COUNTRY OUT OF THE BOY!"

Lessons from Da Farm! YEEHAW!

When I was four years old, my family moved to the farm. The house was on a hill overlooking corn fields and pastures. My dad had cattle, hogs, chickens, and crops. YEEHAAAAW! My older brother, Ryan, was always complaining about how there weren't any malls, movie theatres, or people! Maybe I was too young, but it didn't bother me. Remember, I was the kid who could just sit by himself in the corner and make up an entire imaginary world that kept him happy for many hours. The farm was an amazing opportunity while growing up. It helped me to find myself, appreciate nature, and tell a few stories.

PPR (Professional Pig Riding)

Ya know how girls say, "He swept me off my feet?" Well, I'm about to give that a whole new meaning. I was about six years old, and I was helping my dad in the hog pins. We were separating the younger pigs into different pins. Some people say hogs smell good; they're wrong. Because if they were right, you would walk into those magical candle stores, pick up a big brown candle, look at the sticker, and it would read, "Hog Manure!" and you would get excited, take a big sniff, and say, "Mmm... Hog Manure!" and then pass it around to your friends. But, let's face it. That will never happen!

Anyway, pigs are pigs. They just have a laid-back, "take-it-easy" attitude. They like playing in mud and causing a mess. So, I was standing in the middle of this pig pin, checking out the pigs, when all of a sudden, this little pink pig runs between my legs, picking me up and taking me on a magic carpet ride! Suddenly, I'm in the PBR ring trying to hold on for eight seconds! I was scared out of my mind, probably screaming for my daddy. It all ended up with me on my back in some sludge and trying to hold back the tears.

I usually have meaning and morals to stories, and I bet you're thinking, "What the heck is the point to this story?" Well, check this out. Leadership requires RISK, and if you are going to help others, you need to enter the ring and get in on the action. Sometimes, that means getting knocked around but that comes with RESPONSIBILITY!

Here's a warning. Watch out for pigs (lamesauces) because even though you are trying to help, they can catch you off guard and bring you down to their level. They might not mean anything by it. I mean, pigs will be pigs. But, if you're not careful, you might end up in the mud with them. In other words, people can do stupid things. You can choose to hang out with pigs, but in time, there's a good chance you will probably become one. WARNING: Stay out of the pig pin unless you're going in to clean them off ("helping lamesauces to become awesomesauces").

We risk a lot whenever we don't weigh the pros and cons, consult our head and heart, and make the best decision we can. Trust me, even after doing all of that, you might still make the wrong decision but you'll make far fewer bad decisions if you're a smart risk-taker. A smart risk-taker chooses to make the right decision even if it's not fun. By making right decisions every day, the smart risk-taker gets himself or herself to a place where he or she can do more, be more, and have more fun. Leaders make decisions based on what's right and what needs to be done. We can't expect to get where we want to be if we're not willing to do what it takes. In other words, you can't make it to second base in baseball with your foot still on first. Reflect, prepare, and then take a risk!

Ballroom Dance—in a Wheelchair?

I started ballroom dancing in college, and now I am a certified Ballroom Ninja! Yes, it is that intense. Salsa, swing, tango and about fifteen other dances in total make me a human weapon in the dance world. One of my favorite groups of people to teach is the elderly in retirement centers because when they get out there and dance, their minds forget they're, well, old. You can tell how much they love dancing even though it's mostly shuffling. EVERY DAY I'M SHUFFLING! (Sorry, I had to say that.) In addition to teaching the elderly, I teach students in elementary, middle, and high schools as well as at youth conferences. They learn the dances, but more importantly, they see how teamwork, self-discipline, leadership, courage, and etiquette come about. Each age level is cool in its own way, but all age levels are definitely different in their own way.

Elementary school student: "Dance is awesoooome! Yaayy!"

Middle school student: "I would rather torture myself than dance with the opposite sex.

High school student: (mostly silence) LOL.

I can proudly say that by the end of the lesson everyone loves dance no matter what their age. Why? Aren't most people, especially guys, scared or just not interested in the ballroom dance stuff? Yeah, I think that's right, and I think it's true because they don't see themselves as the type of person who is able to dance. So, they don't like It. Let's face it, most people are not crazy about doing things they think they cannot do. On the other hand, if they start getting good at doing something, they will start liking it. ☺

Back to the question, why do almost all of my students enjoy the lesson? It is because I teach lessons in a way that is simple, funny, and engaging. For example, let's say we're learning a Tango. We start with very simple movements, and I explain them in very simple terms. I also explain in multiple ways because one person might understand with my first explanation while the next person will understand with the second explanation. Next, it's got to be a little bit funny—not taking it too seriously is important. This relieves pressure and allows the students to open up. Last, the moves get slightly harder as the students advance, thus, pushing along their confidence and (drum roll) … fun. Suddenly, they like it because they see themselves able to dance.

Like anything else, whether it's a course in school or band class, the purpose should be to teach in a way that people WANT to learn. Sometimes we don't want to do things, but with the right teacher, anything can be fun and substantive.

Nothing I have done in the dance world has been more fun and substantive than my experience with wheelchair ballroom dance.

I was teaching at an able-bodied studio for about four years when a lady named JoAnne "rolled" through the studio door with her fellow wheelchair dance friends. I was like, "Ummm..." I didn't know what they wanted. I mean, hopefully, not to dance, right?! She introduced herself to all of us and said their organization is called Groovability and they dance ballroom in wheelchairs. I was thinking, "Okay, that's kind of cool... but how?" She said they will stay for the evening party and dance with anyone who was up to it. I couldn't believe it! Talk about risk-takers! The studio was full of able-bodied people who couldn't help but stare, but that didn't scare JoAnne and her friends away.

I'm always up for something new, so I gathered up some courage and walked across the room, but before I could say anything, one of the wheelchair dancers, named Jennifer, wheeled up to me and confidently said, "Hey! Ask me to dance." I was caught off guard. "Uh, okay, but I haven't danced with anyone in a wheelchair." She grinned, "Don't worry; you'll catch on."

We rolled out onto the dance floor, and I took her arms and started to dance like I knew how but quickly realized that I couldn't do a side step with the wheelchair because wheels can't do that. I was doing my very best not to look like a complete idiot.

After a couple of moves I was thinking, "Piece of cake! I can do this." I was at the peak of my confidence and started doing turns and other fancy dance moves with Jennifer. We were dancing fast, and quickly gathering attention from the whole studio. I then remembered a move I knew teaching able-bodied students and thought about how cool it would look with the wheelchair. I pulled her into an inside turn with a cradle wrap and then pulled her backwards as I usually do...

Here's a tip for you all: If you ever find yourself in a situation where you're starting to get real cocky, slap yourself.

Her front wheels came off the ground as I pulled and, like slow motion, I saw a disaster begin to unfold. As she was falling we both simultaneously raised our eyebrows and opened our mouths as if to say, "Ooohhhhh, nooooooo!" She hit the floor with a loud crash and fell out of the chair rolling onto the floor.

Complete silence fell upon the dance studio.

Everyone was staring at her and then at me. (I could tell she was a little upset.) "You can't do that move with a wheelchair," she said, trying to get up. Whoops. All the pride inside me deflated like a punctured balloon. It then hit me that I should help her, so I quickly reached out to help Jennifer get back into her wheelchair. She was still a little distressed. I mean, who wouldn't be? I felt so stupid for trying a fancy move without any practice. I guess that's where you cross the line from smart risk-taking to stupid risk-taking. I apologized, but that didn't make me feel any better. After about twenty minutes of slouching around, like I deserved some type of discipline, Jennifer rolled up to me again and said, "Hey, let's try it again." I couldn't help but smile and graciously accepted her offer. We rolled back onto the dance floor— except this time I took instruction mostly from her.

After that night I realized how much was at risk for me and the dancers, but I was also happy that I worked through my epic dance blunder because that's where most of us fail. When we try something new and it goes terribly wrong, we say, "I'm so stupid for thinking I could do that!" So we never try it again and try fewer new things in the future. You see, this is dangerous because the moment we stop trying and then quit, the next time something similar happens, it's even easier to quit. When we quit, we unknowingly start a habit of quitting. Epic failure is bad, but it's much worse if we don't learn from it and, instead, let it grow like a cancer and make us continuously fail in the future.

I learned from my "bad experience" and continued to practice to make myself better and give dance lessons, eventually becoming the lead instructor for Groovability. My awesome wheelchair dancers included Lorraine Cannistra, Lorie Sparks, Donna Wallis, Jennifer Simmons, JoAnne Fluke, and others. We danced at national competitions and have been featured on a national documentary on *TLC*, *Discovery Health*, and *FitTV*. As wheelchair ballroom dance continues to spread across the country, I continue to be inspired and push to be better. It's true when I hear the quote, "The only true disability is a bad attitude."

In the above story, you can see the leadership quality of being a courageous risk-taker. Courage is a key ingredient in a leader because courage is about pressing on and making the right decision even when you are scared, embarrassed, or uncomfortable. Remember, a lamesauce is someone who doesn't become all that they can, because they're not willing to do all that they need to do. The reason they aren't willing to do it is usually because they're not willing to take responsibility and take a risk. Some people confuse courage with not being afraid, but courage is actually being afraid and still doing it. Even when you land on your back in mud, because of pigs, or when you make a big mistake like I did dancing with Jennifer, you can always learn from it. But, you can't learn from not trying. Stretch yourself by trying something new and, maybe, even a little unfamiliar. It's the only way you'll grow into a true leader.

People Call Me Lem

I was heading back to the "Idaho 4-H Know Your Government" conference for the second year in a row. My first appearance at this conference was awesome. I gave a keynote speech the first night on how _not_ to be a "lamesauce" and then that night I taught swing dance to over 200 youth. The next morning I led a workshop on "Connecting to Your Passion." This year I put together a schedule similar to last year's but with some new material.

The plane touched down in Boise, and after taking a short shuttle ride, I arrived at the hotel. I checked in and got everything unpacked. Students were already showing up, and there was excitement in the air. Some of the students who attended last year's conference quickly remembered me. "Hey, you're the speaker from last year—the 'dance guy'!"

Around 6:30 p.m., while students were gathering outside the conference room waiting for dinner and my speech, I noticed a student standing alone in the corner. He had long brown hair down to his shoulders, and square-framed glasses hung on his nose. There was still some preparation I needed to do, but I felt a strong need to talk to this guy.

As I walked toward him I noticed he had some kind of condition. Later I learned it was Treacher Collins syndrome, a condition in which the facial bones and ear canals don't fully develop. I couldn't help but assume that maybe this was why he was standing by himself. Maybe he didn't know anyone.

I know how much it sucks to feel like an outsider with no one to talk to. It's one of the most uncomfortable feelings, and you just want to escape your body.

"Hey, I'm Brandon, how you doin'?" I asked.

He looked around not sure who I was or why I was talking to him. With a nervous, yet genuine, smile, he looked up. "Hey. People call me Lem."

"Well, good to meet you, Lem! Is this your first year here?"
Quickly he responded, "Uh, yeah."

"Sweet," I replied, making sure I did not crowd him too much. "Are you an eighth grader?"

"Um, yeah, eighth grade."

"Cool, well, I'm speaking tonight and I promise you're going to have a good time."

Lem smiled and looked around anxiously.

"Alright, man," I said, "I'll see you in there."

"See ya," he replied.

After leaving the hallway and entering the conference room I thought about how nice Lem seemed and hoped he would meet people and have a good time. Without giving it further thought, I prepared for my speech. Dinner was served. It was some type of chicken dish, but whatever it was, it was "DELISH!" Plates were eventually removed, and it was now "go time."

I started my speech just as rehearsed and everything was rolling along as planned. Then the part of my presentation came when I would bring up a volunteer who claimed to be a very over-the-top, cheesy actor or actress. Usually, this person would be jumping up and down with a big grin on his or her face—that's the type I look for. So, I asked for a volunteer and, sure enough, there was a guy who "fit the bill."

I said, "Okay, you with the tie on...."

He started to get up, but suddenly, someone right behind him popped up and literally jogged toward the stage. The guy I had called on looked confused and so did the people next to him, but then I realized my mistake.

ALMOST EVERY GUY THERE WAS WEARING A TIE!

Right before this very enthusiastic, mistakenly assumed-to-be volunteer hopped onto the stage, I saw who it was—Lem!

I didn't know what to think. Honestly, on the inside my initial feeling was, "Uh oh." I mean, did Lem really know what I was going to ask him to do? Would he be nervous? Would people laugh at him? These thoughts, however, were interrupted with Lem's beaming smile of confidence. Yeah—confidence. What?

"Okay, here we go," I thought. I went with it and explained that Lem would be acting out a day at school on stage as an "Awesomesauce." He would not talk at all, but instead, I would do the narrating. Without hesitation, he nodded his head as if he had been preparing for this night.

The skit began and I couldn't believe it!

Lem was AMAZING! He was acting out everything with creativity, confidence, and hilarious gestures! People were *laughing so hard and even I was cracking as I narrated. I didn't remember exactly how it happened, but at one point he dragged me into the skit and made everyone almost fall over laughing. At another point, he was to pretend to stick up for someone being bullied, so Lem pretended I was the person being bullied and started stroking my head. By the end of the skit most of the crowd was standing and cheering. It was a standing ovation.*

After Lem sat down, I realized I couldn't stop smiling. In fact, I was holding back the emotion while trying to figure out what had just happened! Then I told everyone, "Out of all the times I have done this skit at schools and conferences, no one—I mean NO ONE—has done it better than how Lem did it just now."

The crowd erupted again in crazy applause.

Then I saw Lem's dad. He also had Treacher Collins. He was sitting down with his arms folded, and had a big smile on his face. I didn't think I had seen a prouder father.

What are the odds that I would have spotted Lem before the conference and talked to him? What are the odds that I would have picked on a student who happened to be right in front of Lem? What are the odds that Lem would have mistakenly thought I picked him? What are the odds that Lem would have surprised everyone and stolen the show?

Honestly, I think there was more than chance involved with what happened.

But, it would not have happened if Lem had not gotten out of his chair. It wouldn't have happened if Lem had not sucked up the courage to stand up and take a risk—even when others doubted him.

But Lem didn't stop there with impressing everyone. After the speech, while the hotel staff was cleaning up the banquet room I walked in to find Lem helping them pick up the dishes and put things away. *This guy is amazing*, I thought. He was later recognized for his character of unexpected service.

Lem is a leader because he took the risk to believe in himself, and he inspired others to have courage. He showed everyone that it's not about the spotlight on stage but about the service when no one is looking.

Thank you, Lem.

RISK

-Author Unknown-

To laugh is to risk appearing the fool.
To weep is to risk appearing sentimental.
To reach out for another is to risk involvement.
To expose your feelings is to risk
exposing your true self.

To place your ideas, your dreams before the
crowd is to risk loss.
To love is to risk not being loved in return.
To live is to risk dying.
To hope is to risk despair.
To try is to risk failure.
But risks must be taken because the greatest
tragedy in life is to risk nothing.
The person who risks nothing does nothing, is
nothing, has nothing.
They may avoid suffering and sorrow but they
simply cannot learn, feel, change, grow, love, live.

Only a person who risks is free.

Risk Takes Courage. Courage Takes Risking.

These stories are about taking risks, but we can't take a risk without having courage. Many people think that to have courage is to not be afraid, but actually, courage is being afraid and doing it anyway.

Courage is a skill that can become a habit. If you do something courageous once then it will be easier to do it twice. Unfortunately, the same is true for fear. If you allow fear to stop you from doing what's right once, it will be easier for it to stop you the next time. Fear is like a supervillain, and courage is like a superhero. Fear can keep us from doing what's right and what needs to be done. Courage is doing what's right and required even if it's scary or unpopular. Fear is the enemy of courage and courage is the enemy of fear. Fear always involves risk, but courage always involves facing that risk.

Fear is not bad. I mean, we fear snakes and spiders for a reason. It's natural. Fear is only bad when we allow it to keep us from making the right decision. Fear is bad when we choose comfort over character. The only way to grow is to face your fears and risk some discomfort.

The good news is that the more you face your fears, the more your fears start to lose their powers. For example, you might have always been afraid of speaking in public, but the more often you do it, the more control you will have over managing that fear. For example, I'm actually afraid of flying, but it's my job to fly around the country and speak. I've realized that if I take a month off, flying is scarier when I come back. If, however, I stay with it then flying isn't so bad.

So, think about what it is that you fear. Maybe it's public speaking or maybe it's a private conversation that you need to have with someone that has been delayed for too long. Maybe it's opening up that past incident that you would rather forget. Maybe it's sticking up for someone. Maybe it's quitting something that has a hold on you. Maybe it's trying out for something you're interested in but afraid of failing at.

Be brave. Take small bites out of your fear each day. Those small victories will eventually add up overtime to something big. Plus, you need to realize that although you live in the United States, you aren't necessarily free. True freedom includes freedom from your fears and negative emotions. When you can choose how to respond the way you want in every situation even when you're afraid...then...THEN...you are closer to true freedom.

Trust = Risk

These stories are also about trust. Jennifer had to trust me that I wouldn't tip her, but I did. I let her down. What do you think that did to her trust in me? She didn't trust me as much anymore. Think about a time when someone let you down and broke your trust. Hurts, right? I know it does. I've let others down, and others have let me down. Whenever we get hurt, our natural reaction is to build walls around us so that no one can hurt us again. And, maybe we won't get hurt again, but we're trapped behind walls. We can't grow. GROWTH TAKES TRUST! Trust takes risk.

There is a smart way and a stupid way to trust. Walking up to a stranger and saying, "Hey, here's my wallet." Umm, probably not a smart way to trust. We have to earn people's trust, but we also have to let people earn our trust. In addition, we help limit the possibility that people will fail us. Jennifer could have helped prevent me from tipping her by saying, "Be careful not to push me too hard when you are holding my hand above my head because I might tip." Prevention is important, but so is forgiveness. Guard your heart but don't trap it behind walls.

Have you ever done the "trust test"? During a conference I called a volunteer to meet me on stage. She was a little nervous because she didn't know what I was going to do. "Leadership involves risk, and it's hard to separate risk from trust." I explained to the audience. "We usually don't risk things unless we trust in those things. For example, I'm not going to eat a certain food un-less I trust it is clean and safe to eat. I'm not going to open up to someone unless I trust that person will listen and empathize with me."

I turned to my volunteer and said, "I'm going to put you through a 'Trust Test', so stand here with your feet togeth-er and arms out. You will fall like a tree, and you can trust me to catch you."

The look on this person's face was priceless.

We counted her down, "3, 2, 1!" She started to fall, and just before she hit the ground, I caught her.

I asked her, "What was the scariest part of that? Was it when you were standing or when you were falling?" She responded that it was when she was falling.

It's scariest when we have **no control.** Whenever we trust someone, we give up some control. All of us have been let down by someone, and when that happens, we have a tendency to build walls so we won't get hurt again. Even though we may not get hurt we're trapped behind our own walls. We cannot grow.

As leaders we have a responsibility to earn people's trust, but we must also allow people to earn our trust. Don't be dumb. Ronald Reagan said, "Trust, but verify." It's the balance between head and heart. Trust can be scary, and that's why it takes courage. Remember, courage is doing the right thing even when you're scared.

Be courageous. Be smart. Earn people's trust. Allow others to earn your trust.

Be ready to catch someone when they're falling.

KEY POINTS:

- Leadership requires RISK, because leadership involves responsibility to do what's right with the potential of failing.

- Growth takes trust. Trust takes risk. Risk takes courage.

- Courage is doing what's right even if it's scary.

- Risk involves fear, and fear is natural, but don't allow it to keep you from doing what needs to and should be done. Be courageous by taking small steps and having encouraging people and resources, like this book!

CHAPTER 4

Lamesauce "Bully" Leadership

-AKA Bully Leadership-

Suddenly, someone appears backstage, "Mr. White, you will be on soon. Are you ready?" I nod and reply, "Yes sir, ready to go." He hurries back out the way he came. I get a little amusement out of his question. One of these times I'm going to have a horrible look on my face and say, "NO! I CAN'T DO IT! PLEASE HEEEELP MEEEEE!" Nah, I wouldn't be mean like that.

Too many people are either lamesauce leaders or they follow lamesauce leaders. People who influence others in a negative way are bully leaders. Bullies are leaders. What? I thought leaders were nice. No, leadership is about influencing people to do something, and bullies are really good at it. Think about it. Bullies even have followers, and they definitely change people's lives. The people we remember the most are the people who make us feel like we're somebody and the people who make us feel like we're nobody. The sad part is that bully leaders are influential, but they're using it in the wrong way. Why do they do this? Bullies bully because of insecurity and a desire to control. Maybe they seek control, because they feel out of control on the inside or at home. Nevertheless, bullies have purpose, and I would like to see them converted to become awesomesauce leaders.

10 Ways to Know If You're a Bully Leader

1. If you expect people to do things a certain way and get mad when they don't, you might be a bully leader.

2. If how nice you are is determined by how much they do what you want them to do, you might be a bully leader.

3. If people rarely open up their feelings to you because they don't feel safe, you might be a bully leader.

4. If you criticize more than compliment, even if it's in your head, you might be a bully leader.

5. If you tell people things more than ask people things, you might be a bully leader.

6. If you get jealous when people follow someone else, you might be a bully leader.

7. If you would rather people follow you and lose than follow someone else and win, you might be a bully leader.

8. If you think respect is expected instead of a privilege that is earned, you might be a bully leader.

9. If you lead just so you don't have to follow, you might be a bully leader.

10. If you don't really like people, you might be a bully leader.

If I'm honest with myself, I was guilty of some of those. I wasn't pushing people down or calling people names, but

I was focused more on myself than others. By my senior year in high school I was student body president, homecoming king, drum major of the band, varsity captain, theatre actor, NHS, Boys' State, SADD... blah, blah, blah.

But, was I really leading anyone? How many people did I truly impact in a positive way? I don't know for sure, but something tells me I was not as much of a "leader" as I thought. Just because I had status and popularity didn't mean I was truly leading. The truth is that, sure, I did some good things and accomplished things. I wasn't a terrible person by any means, but I wasn't a great role model either. I threw parties at my parents' house when they were out of town. You name it, and I probably did it. People see through those masks, and the only person fooled was me. I was a hypocrite.

Bullying has been a big topic at schools for quite some time now. There are programs that schools implement, and they are good, but the truth is that schools can try to decrease bullying or increase the consequences of bullying, but they can't completely stop bullying. People have bullied in the past, they are bullying now, and they will bully in the future. We should try to limit it as much as possible, but if you're trying to make people be nice it's very hard, because you can't make people be nice. What we can control, however, is our individual response to bullying. We need to train students to learn how to respond to bullying instead of reacting. I want you to think of bullies differently. I want you to be more sad for them than mad at them.

Super Brother vs. Super Bully

It was 8th grade track season, and we were all practicing on the track. Since I lived in a small town the high schoolers practiced alongside the middle schoolers. I ran the 400m and 200m sprints. I also tried other events like discus, triple jump, pole vault, and high jump. The only problem was that I couldn't jump high, I couldn't throw far, and pole vault was straight up hard. So, I ran.

There was a junior in high school who was on the track team, and for some reason he didn't like me. One day during practice "junior" came up to me and got right in my face. I just stood there trying to hold my ground. He put his foot behind mine and pushed me down. It happened too fast to think, but all I knew was that I was on the ground with people laughing.

But wait...

There was someone else on the track team who was a senior and he was older, bigger, and stronger than "junior." Oh yeah, and he was MY BROTHER!!!

My brother was a thrower, but that day he came sprinting down towards us after seeing what happened. You see, it was all good now. I just looked up at "junior" and thought, "YOU GONNA GET IT MAN!" My brother got in "junior's" face and stood up for me. "Junior" apologized and was nice to me the rest of practice.

My brother directly and indirectly influenced a lot of people that day. Like a superhero he stood up for me when I couldn't stand up for myself. He was a leader. He helped me directly and inspired others indirectly. I bet even "junior" was influenced, because he looked up to my brother and that day made a big impact on him.

After practice I was riding home with my brother, and before we got home I simply said, "Thanks, man."

Why didn't anyone else on the team stick up for me? What were they afraid of? Sure, they were afraid of junior, but I think they were more afraid of doing what's right when no one else was. It's hard to do what's right when no one else is. That's when you're awesomesauce is tested to see how much you really believe what you believe.

So, what can we learn from my brother? Notice he didn't bully "junior", because that would turn my brother into a supervillain.

*My brother "lifted" junior up by saying, "You're better than that."
Because junior respected my brother before that day, but after that
day he respected him even more. Junior was nicer to me and
everyone after that day, because my brother encouraged him to be
more of an Awesomesauce and less of a Lamesauce.*

My brother's name is Ryan, and he was an awe-somesauce that day, because he chose to be a leader who was willing to accept responsibility despite the risk. Ryan didn't have to help me. It wasn't his fault that Jr. pushed me down. Instead, he chose to take on the responsibility, because he was able to respond and he knew I was worth it.

Another thing I want you to do is to ask the person if they're okay. You probably think I mean the person who is getting bullied. Yes, but I also mean the bully. What? Why? Because, the bully is not okay either. What he did was wrong, but he needs help also. Usually, when we are doing negative things it's because we are feeling negative things. Jr. probably had a lot of negativity inside. Maybe he was bullied when he was my age. Maybe he has an older brother who is mean to him. The possibilities could go on. So, ask the bully this, "Are you OKAY? I saw you push that person down (or whatever they did), why are you angry?" You might be surprised by their answer. Either way, it's important to show them you care, but it's also important to hold them accountable and ask them to stop. "Please don't do that. We wouldn't like it if someone did that to us." Remember, feel more sorry for them than mad at them. If appropriate, you should still report it to a teacher. Some people call that tattling. Tattling is trying to get someone in trouble. Reporting is trying to help someone who is in trouble.

Leaders take time to think about what's really going on, and then they respond with compassion and courage for all people.

KEY POINTS:

- Bully leaders are people who use people for their own gain.

- Be more sorry for someone than mad at them, and then ask caring questions.

CHAPTER 5

Lies of Leadership

There are a lot of lies about leadership. Here are a few:

- Guys are better at leading than girls.
- Leadership is a position such as a president.
- Leadership is getting people to do things.
- Leadership is a personality type you're born with.
- Leadership is for "old" people.
- Leadership means you have to be above people.
- And stuff like that...

Debunking the Myths

- Mother Theresa, Princess Diana, and all the moms in the world are leaders.

- A person's actions and beliefs make himself or herself a leader, not a title. If anything, titles can distract from being "service-centered" to "self-centered." Jesus, for example, was a leader. Yet he did not have an office, let alone a salary, but still was a **very** influential leader.

- Getting people to do things sounds like dictatorship, not leadership. Helping people and empowering people to achieve their goals *is* leadership.

- Leadership is a choice, not a personality trait. Some people think leaders need to be loud and outgoing. Take two people, for example: General Patton and Gandhi. Patton was a U.S. war general during WWI and WWII. His personality/leadership style was very outgoing and assertive (go get 'em, get 'er done, kick 'em in the "you know what"). Gandhi's personality/leadership style, however, was more passive and peaceful. Both were leaders not because of their personalities but because of their principles (having a purpose, serving people, and making a positive difference). They took on risk and responsibility.

- The social network, Facebook, which is one of the largest and most influential companies in the world, was created by Mark Zuckerberg when he was in college. He is now, quite possibly, the youngest most influential person in modern history. You're never too young to be great.

- Leadership is not about being above people; it's about being beside them and pushing them above.

Position and Environment

The problem with understanding leadership is filtering out the gunk associated with leadership. For example, we assume the environment someone is in has to be part of leadership. Leadership is big in the business world, which is a good thing. Therefore, I believe when many people think of leadership they automatically think about bosses, suits and ties, board meetings, and people who oversee other people. Although this is part of the business environment, it is NOT a requirement of leadership.

Another point is that leadership is often associated with a position. People assume a leader is someone, such as a boss or manager, who oversees others. The connection is made, "If I'm not a boss, I'm not a leader." Furthermore, people think a leader needs to "make things happen." As a result people sometimes make the mistake of over-managing to the point where they force instead of lead. Management is about making sure objectives get done through enforcing rules and so forth. However, management becomes dictatorship when leadership is left out. Leadership is the people skills behind management. Leadership empowers others instead of coercing others.

Think of coaching and teaching. Coaches and teachers have a responsibility to enforce rules and cover objectives, but the difference between good coaches and teachers and great coaches and teachers is leadership. Great coaches and teachers get to the heart of the player or student. When people know you care for and respect them, they are more likely to respect you. Nobody likes disappointing someone whom he or she respects and admires. When you are leading with the heart, the rules have a tendency to enforce themselves. For example, let's use parenting. There are all kinds of parents who live in different environments, but the mark of good parents is their ability to lead their children. This requires a balance of encouragement, love, selflessness, counseling, management, and, yes, discipline.

Management asks the question, "Are my children doing what they should, and if not, what discipline is required?"

Leadership asks the question, "Am I doing what I should as a parent to help my child be self-disciplined?"

The Leader Gene?

Have you ever met someone and said, "Man, they were born leaders!" Were they? What do you mean by that? Are they extroverts? Are they charismatic? Does this necessarily make them leaders?

People are born with certain traits and acquire additional traits through the environment in which they live. Someone, for example, might be born with an outgoing personality, which can be advantageous to that person's ability to be a positive risk-taker and to interact with people. It's hard to truly know, though, if someone was born with a personality trait or if he or she acquired it early in childhood. But one thing is for sure. Whether you are born with or have acquired certain traits, it doesn't matter because it's up to you to develop them further and use them.

It's like my old basketball coach used to say, "I'd rather take a player who has mediocre talent, but has an excellent work ethic, over someone who has amazing natural talent and no work ethic." Why? Because whatever you were born with only goes so far, but your potential to work and develop new and existing talents is almost limitless. Even if you have something that doesn't mean you're going to make the most of it.

When I was in elementary school, I struggled with a bad speech impediment. When I talked, people looked at me as though something was wrong with me. They could hardly understand anything I was saying. Do you think that made me want to be more outgoing? No! I started to hate my speech impediment and wished I had not been born that way. I was taken away from my classmates and put into speech therapy. Do you think that made me outgoing? No!

Somewhere along the way I grew out of my speech impediment, and I'll admit, the speech therapy was good for me, except for the annoying sentence I had to practice saying, "The red rabbit ran up the road." It sounded more like, "Da wed wabbit wan up da wode!" Exactly. Somewhere along the way I started to become more out-going and confident. Maybe it was because some real friends came along and cared about me. Maybe it was my loving parents and brother who supported me. Leaders in my life helped to encourage me. But even with all the support, it was up to me to make a decision to be courageous, move forward, and not make excuses. After I was tired of not having friends, I made a decision to take a risk and talk to people.

I was not a born leader. I was shy and had a speech impediment. Some of the other students probably thought I was a complete weirdo. Nobody looked at me and said, "That kid looks like he will make a great leader some day!" I was encouraged by other leaders, and then I chose to develop and grow what was given to me to become the leader I am today. You can, too.

KEY POINTS:

- You have to develop new and existing characteristics.

- Simply having characteristics is not enough. You have to choose to apply them in a way that empowers others.

CHAPTER 6

What is Leadership?

I Thought You'd Never Ask

I check my phone. Everything is right on time, which is amazing considering how much planning goes into these things. Something else I find amazing—the student leaders. In a way, I wish I had been more like them when I was their age. There are some amazing students all over the country that are living out what this book teaches. We need more people like that...

What Student Leaders Think

Before we get into the details of what leadership is, I want to share what some student leaders around the country think about leadership. I asked a few student leaders to discuss their thoughts on a few questions.

1. What are some of the biggest misconceptions about leadership?

"The biggest misconception about leadership is that it is a vehicle to better one's own self-image. Leadership is not about prestige, but rather the ability to positively impact those around you."

Jessica Mullin

Colorado State 4-H - Past President

2. Why do you think leadership is important for the current youth generation?

> *"Today the world is filled with tons of negativity, and that's what most people focus on. That's why I think it's so important for our current youth generation to have positive role models and leaders. We leaders are working hard to bring out the positives and make this world a better place."*
>
> Alex Durham
> Family, Career and Community
> Leaders of America (or FCCLA)
> Past National Vice President of Community Service

3. What needs to be done to help youth develop into better leaders?

> *"Every leader must learn that their decisions, ideas, actions, and words are risks they should be willing to stand for."*
>
> Rendon Corpuz
> Past Alaska FCCLA VP

> *"To help youth develop into better leaders, the current adult and youth leaders need to pass the torch and let new youth leaders practice. The best way to be a better leader is to learn by example and then practice!"*
>
> Kinsey Morley
> Past Colorado District 3 4-H President

"We need to recruit as many teens as possible to a leadership organization, so they stay on the right path and make good decisions."

Kelsie Dawn Kleinschmidt
Oklahoma North District 4 FCCLA
Past Public Relations Officer

These students are right. Leadership is NOT all about a person's self-image and, yes, there is a lot of negativity in our culture that misrepresents leadership. In addition, I agree we need to promote our leadership organizations and CTSOs so that we can help students become awesomesauces.

Leadership is a powerful topic that can be expanded and presented in many ways. The focus can be on the definition of leadership, the application of leadership, the impact of leadership, the various leadership styles and strategies, and on and on and on. Where do we start? Let's start by recapping what we've covered so far. We started with taking ownership of who we are and the fear that holds us back from being our true selves. Then, we discussed the essential factors of responsibility and risk when accepting a leadership role. Finally, we mentioned the lies of leadership and what leadership is not.

"The 3 Cs of Leadership"

Character, Competence, and Courage.

Character (Be It): If people are to follow you they need to know they can trust you.

Competence (Know It): They also need to know that you know what you're talking about.

Courage (Do It): They need to know that you won't back down when it gets tough.

Leadership starts with character. Sure, you can be a dictator leader, but then you're just a lamesauce. Think of character as the foundation to your leadership. Character is all the good things you would want in a friend. Would you want a friend to be dishonest, disloyal, disrespectful, irresponsible, untrustworthy, etc.? Nope. Character is all the good things about someone originating from love and virtues. Having good character requires living with virtues. Discipline, honesty, trustworthiness, respect, loyalty, and responsibility are all examples of virtues and good character.

Awesomesauce = others-centered (character)
Lamesauce = self-centered (lack of character)

We develop character from seeing it modeled for us. Of course, it's easier to create character in children than adults, because children are more impressionable. As we get older our habits are formed along with our character, and it's harder to change. Nevertheless, the hardest of hearts can be changed at any age, and the thing that does it is love. When someone is honest, genuine, loyal, respectful, generous, and compassionate, we can't help but feel loved. We let down the walls around our heart and start to feel again. We want to love back, because humans weren't just made for learning, building, and reproducing. They were made to be loved and to give love. To love others who are not like you, or who don't even like you is the most powerful force in existence. It has the power to turn bad into good.

But the 3Cs alone is not leadership. It's about how the 3Cs are used. You see, leadership is about empowering others, which means to *help others help themselves.* You are only truly leading when you are helping others see what they can't see and achieve what they want to achieve because of your guidance and support.

EMPOWER: The Goal of Leadership

To empower is to endow, enable, and invest. Ultimately, it's means to help others help themselves. This is different than influence because influence doesn't imply that you inspired someone to be better. For example, I can influence someone by being forceful or violent but that's not leadership. I can influence someone by letting them cheat off of my test answers but that's not leadership. A basketball coach doesn't shoot the basketball for you. Instead, he teaches you how to shoot and encourages you to believe in yourself so you have the courage to take that last-second shot on your own. That's the ultimate influence—empowerment. This is also the goal of parents and teachers. They teach you what they know to help you become better, but the ultimate sign of their effectiveness is if they have empowered you to continue bettering yourself on your own.

How exactly do we empower people? Should you do the work for them? No. Should you boss them into doing what they need to do? No.

I created a simple illustration that is easy to understand. This will help you understand the actions of leadership and its purpose to empower. When you finish this book, I want you to be able to describe to someone what leadership is in one sentence. What I've found with speaking around the country is that MOST PEOPLE CAN'T DO IT! Isn't that amazing? We need to make it simple so you can make it happen.

SUPER LEADER

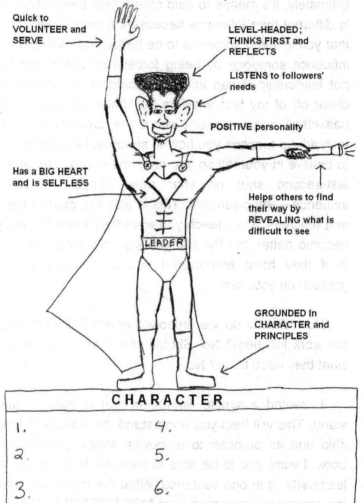

Quick to VOLUNTEER and SERVE

LEVEL-HEADED; THINKS FIRST and REFLECTS

LISTENS to followers' needs

POSITIVE personality

Has a BIG HEART and is SELFLESS

Helps others to find their way by REVEALING what is difficult to see

GROUNDED in CHARACTER and PRINCIPLES

LEADER

CHARACTER

1.

2.

3.

4.

5.

6.

Yes, I know this is very cheesy and almost painful to look at. But, it will now be imprinted in your mind forever! Muahahaha!

Listed beneath the "Super Leader" diagram are numbers one through six. Next to each number, write down an example of character (i.e., loyalty, honesty, etc.). These characters are the foundation of leadership. If you're having trouble thinking of 6 examples of character, you can cheat by looking at the character section in the pages to come. (And no, cheating is <u>not</u> an example of character!)

Now, let's briefly describe each "Super Leader" action/trait:

Volunteer: Name three examples of how you willingly volunteered to do something for someone without any reward attached to it. When was the last time you went out of your way or gave up something for someone else? When have you taken the time to help someone by listening and getting involved with his or her life?

For me, I realized that before I became a seasoned "awesomesauce" I couldn't list many times when I truly volunteered. And, I'm not talking about some community service you get extra credit in class for doing. I'm talking about true selfless "nothing-initially-in-it-for-you-except-pure-love service."

You might say, "That's awkward or I don't have time."

Listen to me; it's awkward because you're making it awkward, and you don't have time because you don't want to make time. Truth! There are a ton of websites that you can browse that list all the community service opportunities in your area. Search "community service opportunities" and start checking out those websites. Find one that seems cool and get some friends to do it with you. Seriously, put your bookmark in and go on that website right now... or do it tonight. After you do it and found it to be so rewarding you can email me and say, "I thought it was going to be lame, but you were right. BEST TIME OF MY LIFE." Just like that with all the caps and stuff. Let's recap. Community service is like drugs except that it is legal, way less harmful, and I actually promote it unlike drugs. What I'm saying is that it is addicting and you will want to do it again... OK... moving on.

Besides, you can also serve in others way. Offer to help out at a local store or business that you have an interest in. Another option is to help at a nursing home or simply spending some extra time at your own grandparents.

> **Level-Headed:** Being level-headed takes maturity. It's easy for someone to react emotionally because of lust, jealousy, humor, boredom, and so on. You have reached maturity when you can say to yourself,

"Reacting is often absorbing someone else's negative reaction and shooting it right back. That's what babies do. If you smile, the baby will usually smile back. If you make a monster face, the baby will get upset, scream, and cry like a... baby."

Responding, on the other hand, is based on character. Your response is not dictated by the other person's reaction. Your response is not based on revenge or venting your anger. It's based on self-control and doing the right thing unlike the out-of-control emotional hurricane of a "lamesauce."

Vision: Part of being level-headed is having a vision. Vision is the map before the exploration. Vision is choosing where you want to go and why before you pack. Vision pertains to the future, not just today. Vision provides inspiration, because it gives not just the goal, but the reason for wanting to achieve that goal. A leader should include the follower or team in the vision process. Ask them, "What do you want and why?" "What does it look like specifically?"

Think about the vision Mark Zuckerberg, the founder of Facebook, had. What he created was a way for people to connect with others, express themselves, and change the way communication and advertising is now done. His vision was selective, inclusive, and satisfied needs. He followed up his vision with action plans so that the vision of Facebook would continue to survive and thrive. They also bought Instagram in 2012, because Facebook could see the vision of Instagram's success. By the way, you can find me on social media at "Youthmover".

My vision for myself is to help youth take ownership of

who they are, what they want, and what holds them back through teaching leadership and character skills.

In order to do that, I will seek consistent improvement in my content, marketing, and business operations so that I can maintain a profitable and sustainable business. I will seek others' opinions and help. I will strive to maintain balance in my business and personal life so that I do not get burned out or neglect my family. I will continue to evaluate my vision and even adjust it as necessary to ensure I am going in the right direction.

So, as you can see I had a Vision Statement followed by some Action Plans to make it happen. Think about what the big vision for your life is. Think big, but don't forget the details to make it happen.

> *"Leadership is the capacity to translate vision into reality."*
>
> –Warren Bennis (American Scholar)

Listen: You can always tell when people are not really listening. When my wife and I were dating, she busted me one day when she was going on and on about this huge emotional story about girl stuff, and then, out of nowhere, she turned, looked right at me, and asked, "What did I just say?" OH, MAN! This was the worst! She knew I wasn't listening and called me out on it. So I was left staring at her like some helpless puppy that was caught with the shoe in his mouth. Not fair!

The most important thing about listening is that you make the other person feel understood.

- Don't be distracted by your phone or other people. You don't have to stare into their eyes the whole time, but don't let them think that you would rather be doing something else.
- Quality over quantity. It's okay if you're not a big talker or socializer, but whatever you do, make it count.
- Don't be quick to give advice or talk about yourself. Instead, ask more questions like "who, what, when, where, why?"
- Validate their feelings such as, "I bet you were so upset..." "I bet you were so excited..."
- Listen more than you talk.
- Silence is okay. Questions are the best way to break the silence.

It's also important for a leader to listen to others' advice and take feedback. If you do this, they will respect you more, and you will grow from it. If someone is giving you advice or an opinion that you disagree with, first make them feel understood. "I hear what you're saying. What would you have me do? Even if we disagree, I want to be respectful to your opinion." Listen without getting defensive is the best way to remove anger. Even if people don't come to you first, ask them for their opinion. It shows that you respect what they think.

"People don't care how much you know until they know how much you care."

–Anonymous

Positive Attitude: Have you ever heard the saying "Success is comprised of 80 percent attitude and 20 percent skill"? There is a lot of truth in that. Remember the story about my wheelchair dance students? JoAnne, for example, was born with Caudal Regression, a condition where her legs didn't grow, leaving her practically with no legs. Even though she doesn't have legs, she still maintains a positive attitude. She is determined to be as independent as she can. Whenever she is not using her wheelchair, she walks on her hands. She can't reach the bathroom countertop so she brushes her teeth in the tub by using the faucet. She can't just open her vehicle door and step inside. Instead, she gets in through the back of her station wagon by opening the back door, crawling out of her wheelchair onto the floor board of the car, pulling her wheelchair inside and then crawling over each seat, finally landing in the driver's seat where she drives the car using special hand-operated controls. Now, don't you feel lazy? Yeah, I feel pretty lazy, too, every time I see her do this, which is about every week after we finish dancing. Just like all my wheelchair dance students, JoAnne inspires others with her positive attitude on life and her willingness to take responsibility rather than make excuses.

Another wheelchair student of mine, Lorraine Cannistra, wrote a poem about her challenge with Cerebral Palsy and her choice to keep a positive attitude, anchored in her faith. Her positive attitude perspective is why, I believe, she is not only a leader but an awesome person.

SIMPLY THE FRAME

By: Lorraine Cannistra

Sometimes I feel trapped inside
My prison of four wheels
People say they understand
But they don't know how it feels
I don't want to be treated differently
I don't want special care
Why won't people treat me like me
Instead of a person in a chair
I feel so sad and lonely
And I'm a bit confused
Of all people who could have had C. P.
Why was it me God had to choose?
His answer comes so gently
I've known it all along
"I didn't choose you to be cruel, my child,
I chose you because you're strong
Think about the someday soon
When we'll be side by side
I'll watch you walk so gracefully
My heart will swell with pride
And even though in this life on earth
Your situation may never change
In the beautiful picture I've painted of you
Your wheelchair is simply the frame."

Help Others Find Their Way: This is the bread and butter behind leadership.

Volunteering, having a level head, listening, and having a positive attitude are all very important, but the essence of leadership is EMPOWERMENT! If you are doing all those things but not empowering anyone, you're not being a Super Leader.

Look at the flashlight in the diagram. What does light do? It reveals what is not, otherwise, seen. This relates to the vision character we talked about earlier. A flashlight helps you see ahead, but without it you are simply stumbling aimlessly in the dark. There's a difference, though, between helping others find their way and trying to make them go your way. The second method is selfish and doesn't involve empowerment.

Think of your parents. Now, I'm not out to bash parents, and remember you, too, might be a parent one day. Nevertheless, parents have a tendency to try to light "the way" instead of helping their children find "their way." Have your parents ever said that they know what is best for you? Did they try to "show you the way"? How did that go? It might not have turned out positive since nobody likes feeling like a brainless puppet. Although parents might have the best intentions and their way might have been the best way, they may not have been effective because their approach was wrong. The common mistake is made when people think that leadership is "lighting the way." On the contrary, leadership is "helping others find

THEIR way." For example, let's say that Tina approaches Jill and says, "Jill, I just got cut from the soccer team." Jill decides to light the way for Tina and responds, "You need to forget about soccer and try out for basketball. While you're at it, you need to go out with the Brad boy because he is super-duper cute and has an Australian accent. There you go!" Jill feels like she is such a leader!

Although Jill went about it with good intentions, Tina probably doesn't feel understood and thinks that Jill only looks at her as a problem that needs to be fixed. Ladies, I feel like I must take this time to apologize for the entire male population because we can be bad at this. Just because somebody is going through something difficult doesn't mean you are supposed to tell them what to do and fix it for them. Instead, they need a friend who will listen, ask questions, give support, and provide suggestions. Just because somebody is opening up doesn't mean they want you to tell them what to do. The first desire and need to fill is their need to feel understood. How do you do that? Ask questions and listen. For example, what if Jill responded, "You got cut from the team? What happened?" (That's a perfect start.)

Your first priority is to let them know you care by listening to them with a level head, positive attitude, and a big heart. Let the other person vent and explain what he or she is thinking and feeling. This will help him or her gain perspective for himself or herself. You can then ask, "So, do you think you're going to try again next year, or are you thinking about going out for a different sport?" And <u>always</u>

finish with them knowing you are a real friend who supports them, not someone who knows how to live their life better than they do. "Well, I'm here for you for whatever. I don't know exactly how it feels, but I know if it happened to me, I would also want someone to talk to."

So, to help people find their way, you don't need to preach to them. Instead, help them by showing them they can trust you to listen and not judge. Then, ask questions that will help them think about it in a way they never have before. You will, ultimately, help them find their success and happiness through asking questions, providing support, and gaining clarity.

Big Heart: A Super Leader has a big heart for people and for doing the right thing. It's not hard to detect compassion, but sometimes it's hard to find. You see, when someone has a big heart, he or she SHOWS it. It's one thing to say, "Of course, I care about you." It's another thing to show it. A Super Leader shows love by giving his or her time and attention. Most of the time, we don't go out of our way to show it. Why? It's easier to be selfish; it's harder to be selfless. You can't fake a big heart because it's not a one-time thing. It's a lifestyle choice to choose to put others first and to give out of love. By doing that, trust me, you get much more in return.

Now, I'm not trying to preach to anyone, but I can't think of anyone who would be a better example of having a big heart than my main man, Jesus. Whether you believe him to be the savior or not, you have to admit, he was one heck of a person. He is a perfect example of a Super Leader. I mean just look at what he DID!

Jesus was so ridiculously awesome that he continuously chose to help people even if they did nothing for him. He taught to love your neighbor AND your enemy. Think about it; would a super leader hate a super lamesauce? NO! A super leader loves that person even if the super leader hates the bad choices that the super lamesauce makes. The super leader still cares about the super lamesauce. Don't hate the person; hate the lame choices the person is making.

Love means having patience with people and forgiving them instead of holding grudges. When you refuse to forgive someone, you hurt yourself more than the other person. You carry your bitterness and pain around like a weight, keeping you stuck in the past and robbing you of your future. So many people have a hard time letting go of a "wrong-doing" by someone else. I once had a very, VERY big grudge of bitterness and pain toward someone who hurt me in the past. It consumed me like a cancer and affected everything else I thought about and did. One day I realized how tiring and pointless my hurt and hate were. I chose to forgive. It was as though a weight was removed because I was no longer trying to be "the judge" of deciding what was fair. Instead, I admitted that no one is perfect, and it's not so much about me as it is about something personal that the other person might be going through that makes that person act that way.

When you truly love people, you will forgive them.

You will want the best for them.

You will be sad more about how they are acting than mad about how it's not fair.

Don't be a like a baby who reacts to negativity with negativity. The answer is always the same: Respond with love.

Leadership Summary

What is leadership?

1. **WHAT:** EMPOWERING - Helping others help them-selves. A person empowers by demonstrating, encouraging, listening, and supporting until they can do it on their own. Be careful that you're not doing things for them and stealing their opportunity to grow. If the teacher took the test for you, it would defeat the true purpose of making you smarter. The teacher's responsibility is to empower you so that you can pass the test on your own.

2. **HOW:**
   - Cs- (Character, Competence, and Courage)
   - Using SUPER LEADER actions: (level head, posi-tive attitude, listen, big heart, help others find their way, and grounded in character.)

3. **WHY**: RISK and RESPONSIBILITY - that comes with leading.

Leadership is empowering others through character, com-petence, and courage using Super Leader actions despite risk and because responsibility. THAT'S IT!

That's a basic understanding of what leadership is and how it applies to YOU! You see, not everyone is going to be the boss of a company or the president of a club, but they don't have to be "to be a leader." Why? Anyone can acquire these "Super Leader" qualities. These are not qualities that you have to be born with. These are qualities you choose to do!

THINGS TO REMEMBER WHILE LEADING

The Emotional Bank Account

In order to further understand leadership, it's important that we distinguish between direct and indirect leadership. Great leaders do both. Direct leadership is one-on-one influence with someone based on what you say or do to them. Coaches, teachers, bosses, and parents are examples of positions that require direct leadership. Do you need to have that position in order to be a direct leader? No. If you are utilizing the "Super Leader" model to help a friend overcome a challenge, you are being a direct leader.

Indirect leadership is influencing others based on their observation of you. You don't even have to know the people or meet them to indirectly lead them. Think of a true story you heard that inspired you to be a better person. Maybe that story encouraged you not to give up, or maybe it showed you that you have more potential than you think. Whatever the reason, that person's story indirectly influenced you. That person indirectly helped you to help yourself. Even though the two of you never met, THAT PERSON EMPOWERED YOU!

I believe we are called to be both direct and indirect leaders. We have a responsibility to work with people one on one, and we also have a responsibility to indirectly lead people by living our lives with courage and responsibility. Through living our lives with passion and purpose we help influence others to do the same.

Think of it this way, you are already directly and indirectly influencing people. The question is, "When people think of you, what do they think?" Do they think this person is courageous or cowardly, authentic or fake, kind or cold, trustworthy or untrustworthy, honest or dishonest, responsible or irresponsible?

You shouldn't worry about what people think about you or be someone you are not only to please others. However, you should strive to maintain a positive "authentic" image not because you're faking it but because you're living it.

How are you _indirectly_ influencing people? How are you _directly_ influencing people?

The Emotional Bank Account

One of my favorite books is Stephen Covey's *7 Habits of Highly Effective People*. In it, Stephen talks about the Emotional Bank Account. Whenever I praise someone, give positive feedback, spend quality time, or make them feel understood I am making an emotional deposit. On the other side, whenever I confront someone, ask for a favor, give advice, or create conflict I am making an emotional withdraw. Just like a real bank account, you want to have more deposits than withdraws. If you have more deposits, you will be rich, but if you have more withdraws than deposits you will be broke. The same is true with relationships. You can ask for favors or give advice, but make sure you have sufficient funds. Make sure you have deposits of listening, supporting, encouraging, spending time, etc. People don't like to follow leaders who make too many withdraws, and when you make deposits with others they will want to deposit into you.

(Positive) Deposits: compliments, support, encouragement, listening, spending time, doing favors, etc.

(Negative) Withdraws: Giving advice, asking for favors, offering critique, lying, etc.

Sharpen the Saw

Have you heard the saying, "You only get what you put into it"? Think of it this way. We want more while spending less. We want quicker results with less effort. Part of that is smart, and part of that is lazy. The way that you are going to get more for less in life is by working smarter with very efficient tools. I love Stephen Covey's book, 7 *Habits of Highly Effective People*, because it talks about "sharpening the saw." If you were given a job to cut down a big tree and you could either get to work right away with a dull axe or spend time sharpening the axe and then cutting, which would you do? The truth is if you cut with the dull axe it will take ten times as long and you will be ten times as frustrated versus if you take the time up front to sharpen your axe before cutting. But, what do people say? "I don't have time. I don't want to do that. That's no fun."

Reading this book is helping you sharpen your tools to become a more effective leader. Why? So you can make a bigger, more positive difference in your life and the lives around you. Like an axe, your life needs to be more effective at slaying the fear, ignorance, and other bad things that keep you from happiness and success.

It's worth the time sharpening.

KEY POINTS:

- Empower: Helping others help themselves

- 3 Cs: Character, Competence, and Courage.

- Super Leader: level head, positive attitude, listen, big heart, help others find their way, and grounded in character.

- Choose to be a leader despite risk and because of responsibility.

- Direct leadership is the one-on-one influence towards a specific goal, and indirect leadership is influencing others based on their observation of you. We are called to be both, so choose your words and actions wisely no matter where you are.

- Make more positive deposits into people's emotional bank accounts than negative withdraws.

- Learn this stuff so that you have a sharper axe to make a bigger impact.

CHAPTER 7

Leadership Personalities

I text my wife almost every time before I go on stage. She has been there for me through it all even when I just started and didn't know if anyone would hire me. Support is so important, because if you're like me you can have some doubts. My wife says, "I would hate your job!" Haha, she is more of a "steady job" person that doesn't require public speaking. But, you know, I wouldn't want her job, either. She works in a hospital. It takes all types.

Chapter 4 mentioned that leadership is not a personality trait. You can have soft and quiet leaders. You can have bold and loud leaders. Extroverts can be leaders and so can introverts. Unfortunately, many people are trying to be what they're not, because they think they have to be a certain person to be a leader. I have a Master's in Business and a Major in Psychology, but my favorite has always been psychology. To "know thyself," as the Greeks believed in is so important, but so is seeking to know others. This chapter will help you discover your personality type as well as others and be able to have a greater impact. It will also help you identify potential negative personality traits that sabotage leadership.

Personality Test

In the blank spaces, rank the personalities in order 1-4, with 1 being what you associate with the most and 4 being what you associate with the least. Use each number only once. Next, circle your top 3 of strengths in each personality.

_____ **The "Strong-Willed":** Gets things done, wants to give their best, and loves accomplishing goals.

Strengths: Efficient, Effective, Competitive, Disciplined

_____ **The "Woohoo!":** Enjoys having fun as a group, engaging others, and making sure work is fun.

Strengths: Sociable, Engaging, Positive, Energetic, Fun

_____ **The "Is Everyone Okay?":** Cares about other's well-being, making sure the group is okay, and resolving conflict.

Strengths: Listening, Encouraging, Empathizing, Loyal

_____ **The "Deep Thinker":** Enjoys understanding the big picture, being creative, and reflecting on deeper issues.

Strengths: Reflective, Creativity, Analytical, Logical, Problem-Solving

MY CODE: ___ ___ ___ ___

There is no "right" code. Each personality has different strengths that can help different people in different situations. You can try to grow your weaker personalities, but don't spend too much time trying to be something you're not. Acknowledge your weaknesses and improve on them, but don't get stuck on them. Accentuate strengths, because that is what makes you.

For example, if you're not a "Woohoo," at all, then that might hurt your leadership because you won't be fun to be around. On the other hand, if you try too hard to be fun and funny, it will come off as fake. Try this, hang out with the people who naturally have those traits. We often become more like the people we hang out with. In the end, you have to do you, because no one else can.

People usually think I am a "Woohoo!" because when they see me at speeches, my energy is up and my jokes are funny. Hahaha, that's funny. Because, "Woohoo!" is my last place. I'm a "4,1,3,2." My natural personality is reflective, creative, driven, and compassionate. I've had to learn to bring that "Woohoo!" side of me out, because if I want to be a good motivational speaker, I need to be fun and funny. Now, if I was just fun and funny with no substance then that's not good either. I start fun and funny and then move into serious, because I've heard it said that the shortest distance between two people is humor. When people are laughing they are more likely to listen and trust you. In fact, I specifically design my speeches so that they include all four personality types to reach all people, while at the same time remaining true to who I am. The point is to stretch yourself, learn from others, and stay true to your core personality.

I ask students to raise their hands if their number one personality is "Strong-Willed." At first I thought most people would be strong-willed, especially if it's a leadership conference. Instead, everywhere I go and no matter the size of the group about 25% are "Strong-Willed," 25% are "Woohoo!" 25% are "Are You Okay," and 25% are "Deep Thinker." What does that tell you?

It tells you that we are diverse, and we are diverse for a reason. I believe the human species was meant to work together, and if everyone had the same personality they couldn't help each other and make up for each other's' weaknesses. Unfortunately, this is also the reason for a lot of conflict, because people misunderstand each other. A "Woohoo!" might think a "Deep Thinker" doesn't want to have fun with them or isn't paying attention. Likewise, a "Deep Thinker" might think the "Woohoo!" isn't taking things seriously. This is why empathy is so important. If we stop to think about where the other person is coming from we will prevent conflict, become more likeable, have more fun, and become better leaders.

It also tells you that leaders can be all types of personalities. The point is to use your personality in the framework of "empowering others through volunteering, thinking with a level head, having a positive attitude, listening, having a big heart, helping others to find their way, and being grounded in character despite risk and because of responsibility."

Dark Personalities

Behind each personality trait is a dark side that comes out when we lack character. Not only are they harmful when you demonstrate them, but they are also harmful when you don't respond to other people's dark personalities in the right way. For example, if someone yells at us we might want to yell back or shut down. If someone brags of manipulates, we might want to put them down or punish them back. Other people's dark personalities can bring out our dark personalities. This is why we have to be aware of them and control them before they control us.

As you look at the dark personality types on the next page, ask yourself the following questions:

1. Which one am I most like?
2. Which one can my family members, classmates, team-mates, or teachers be?
3. Which one makes me more defensive or hurt when done to me?
4. What brings out my dark personality?
5. What, maybe, brings out the dark personality of the people mentioned above?

The Dark Personalities

 THE EXPLODER: Short-tempered, easily offended, defensive, lacks self-control, lacks empathy, competitive. Explodes when they don't get their way or when disrespected.

 THE COMPLAINER: Negative, avoids responsibility, can be lazy, entitled, self-centered. Complains when things get difficult. Can also be a blamer.

 THE SCHEMER: Witty, manipulative, dishonest, deceiving. Schemes for their own personal gain at the expense of others. Says one thing, does another thing. Spreads rumors.

 THE PEOPLE-PLEASER: Unhealthy desire to be liked, because they are afraid of being disliked. They will be different things to different people to be liked by everyone, but usually ends up with people not respecting them or knowing who they really are.

 THE BRAGGER: Cares about their own achievements and good qualities. They are self-absorbed, and they usually have hidden insecurities.

 THE DISTANCER: Retreats into their thoughts and feeling while pushing people away. Shuts down. Lacks trust.

You might be able to think of more dark personalities, but this is a good start. So, what causes dark personalities? Who we are is made up of our nature (what genetics we're born with) and our nurture (how we are raised and what environments we experience). For example, I believe some people are born with a bigger temper and others are born with a tendency to distance themselves. If they are put in an environment with peers and parents that do the same things then you have the perfect situation for a dark personality to be deeply ingrained in that person. Regardless, dark personalities are expressed because of selfishness, laziness, jealousy, insecurity, arrogance, and other unhealthy behaviors.

Just because we have a tendency to get mad, complain, etc. doesn't mean we have to act on it. Self-control is the mark of maturity, and it's like a muscle, the more you practice it the stronger it gets. Really, it's a habit. Habits are formed by repeatedly doing something until it becomes ingrained. Unfortunately, the old negative habits (dark personalities) are stronger than the new habits. Also, we usually do things because we feel like it. "They made me 'feel' mad, so I yelled." "They hurt my feelings, so I quit." Maturity is doing what's right even if you don't feel like it. I often say in my speeches that doing what's wrong might feel good at first, but usually hurts afterward. Doing what's right might hurt at first, but usually feels good afterward. This is the concept of delaying gratification and it's what practicing a sport or studying for a test is all about.

How to Respond to Dark Personalities

Awesomesauces take time to stop and think about what they're feeling before reacting out of a negative feeling. Lamesauces don't respond, they just react with how they feel, and because of that, they have a hard time developing positive habits and living a healthy and successful life. So, how should you respond to the dark personalities? What should to say or do? Here are some guidelines:

Exploder: They want to feel heard and respected, so give them that. It doesn't mean you to have to agree with them or do what say. When we get angry, the part of our brain that is logical shuts down, so if we ask questions and listen the brain will have time to reboot.

Key Questions: Ask for specifics. "Give me an example. When did that happen? What exactly did they say or do? What do you want to happen now?" Make them feel understood by clarifying. "I want to understand where you're coming from. Are you saying that…?"

Complainer: They want results, but they usually don't want to help provide them. If they're going to complain make them accountable to be part of the solution.

Key Questions: "I hear that you don't like how this person is doing this. Do you want to come with me to talk with them so we can figure this out?" "I hear that you don't like how we're doing this. What would you suggest we do differently?"

Schemer: They are flat out sneaky, and they usually put their interests before others. Hold them accountable with a private conversation instead of a public scolding.

    Key Questions: Be specific. "I saw that you did/said _____ on this particular day, and I was disappointed because it seems like you were trying to _____, and I don't think of you as that kind of person. Did I misunderstand this?" Even if they lie to you, they will respect you for how you addressed it and that might encourage them to change.

People-Pleaser: They want to be liked, they dislike conflict, and they usually lack self-esteem. These people are usually not mean. Although their actions damage relationships, they are also victims of their own doing. Let them know you like them for them and encourage them to be themselves.

    Response: "I wanted to talk to you about something, because I'm your friend. I'm worried that you aren't being yourself. I saw you say/do _____ and that doesn't seem like you. I just want you to know that you can always be yourself around me."

Bragger: They want to feel important. They may or may not know that they're doing it. Respond to them the same way as you would a Schemer. Be careful. Only confront them if it's truly necessary, because it could cause more harm than good. Regardless, always be gentle and respectful.

<u>Distancer:</u> They don't like conflict, which is why they run from it. These people are usually not mean. Although their actions damage relationships, they are also victims of their own doing. Let them know you care and respect their privacy.

Response: "You don't have to talk to me if you don't want to. I'm not trying to force you. I just wanted to let you know that I care, and I don't like to see how this has such a negative effect on you. What did they say/do? What happened? If you don't want to talk, I understand, just wanted to be here for you…"

Let your light shine on the dark or the dark might overtake you.

Awesomesauce leaders know themselves, control themselves, develop themselves, and give of themselves for the sake of others doing the same.

"An unexamined life is not worth living."

-Socrates (Greek Philosopher)

"Diversity may be the hardest thing for a society to live with, and perhaps the most dangerous thing to live without."

-William Sloane Coffin Jr. (Peace Activist)

"Remember that everyone you meet is afraid of something, loves something and has lost something."

-H. Jackson Brown Jr. (Author)

KEY POINTS:

- Acknowledge your weaknesses and improve on them, but don't get stuck on them. Accentuate your strengths, because that is what makes you.

- Learn to identify others' personalities and dark personalities so that you can relate to them.

- Let your light shine on the dark or the dark might overtake you.

- Awesomesauce leaders know themselves, control themselves, develop themselves, and give of themselves for the sake of others doing the same.

CHAPTER 8

Show Some Love

The teacher begins reading my bio. "My bio is too long," I'm thinking to myself as the teacher takes a breath and continues reading. Bios are kind of funny. How do you write a bio without sounding completely egotistical? You want to be professional, but it's like, "Hey, look at all I did so that I'm worthy of talking to you." If my bio said, "Brandon likes to watch YouTube and eat chocolate," would anyone hire me? :)

It's almost show time. This is when I start feeling the energy, say a quick prayer, and get ready to kick tail!

People ask me what I like most about my job, and without a doubt, I have to say, "It's when people come up to me or write to me and tell me how much my speech has helped them." That feels good.

But you know, this whole "Youth Mover" thing and traveling across the country can be dangerous because I know how easy it is to let things get to your head. All of a sudden you can think you're some super cool, kind-of-celebrity person. That's a leader's challenge, especially if he or she is given a special title or gains popularity and status because of his or her title.

Leaders need to show some love! Leaders are others-centered, not self-centered. They take time to listen and understand instead of blabbing and seeking to be understood. It's a choice, but the difference between the right and wrong choice is a little discomfort, which takes courage.

Good Pizza

Have you ever pulled up to a stoplight and there's a homeless man standing on the corner with a sign in his hands? He's standing right next to your car, and your car is the only one in sight. He is looking directly at <u>you</u>, and it's just straight up awkward. You try not to make eye contact while waiting for the light to turn green. I had always wondered if these people were really in need of help or if they were just lazy and trying to bum money for drugs. Well, I have several stories I can share with you about my personal relationship with homeless people but I'll just share this one:

I just got into Raleigh, North Carolina, and checked into the hotel. I was going to speak the next day at the North Carolina State FFA Conference with 3,000 youth attending. I was hungry for some local grub, so I headed out on foot to look for a local restaurant. After passing about ten different restaurants, nothing was really catching my eye. There were fancy restaurants, cafés and bars, but I kept walking, still hopeful to find the right one. Suddenly, I came across a pizza joint, and I saw a man standing in front of the building. He walked up to me and said, "Excuse me, sir, I'm not asking for money, but I was hoping you could help me get some pizza for my family."

Well, well, well, here's an interesting situation. This guy "supposedly" is not homeless, but he is in need. He doesn't want money. He wants food. He's doesn't want food just for himself but for his family supposedly.

Listen, this is what I decided in life some time ago: There are times when you cannot be 100 percent sure that what you're doing is the right thing. So I had decided that if I'm going to be wrong, I'd rather be wrong because I gave... than be wrong because I didn't give.

"Sure, man. Let's go inside and get some pizza. What's your name?"

"Anthony. Thank you so much, man; I really appreciate it."

So, we head in, and Anthony's clothes and appearance are borderline "bummish" and the pizza worker can detect this. "That's good," I thought. "People need to see people helping people."

"Alright, what looks good to you, Anthony?"

"Ohh, anything would be fine...just a small sausage pizza or something."

"You sure? I like a lot of toppings."

He perked up, seeing a golden opportunity, "Well, uh, yeah, I like pretty much all the toppings, too!"

"Hey, how about we get an extra-large supreme pizza? I'll take a couple of slices and you can have the rest."

Anthony was stunned and after a couple seconds of silence he smiled saying, "Okay."

So I ordered this humongous, "expensive" pizza, and we took a seat to wait for it.

This is the moment. Look, more than money or food, people need to know others care about them. Sometimes, it's easier to drop some change into someone's hand than to spend ten minutes talking to them because the difference between right and wrong usually brings a little discomfort, which takes courage.

Anthony and I started talking. I learned that he had worked at a local plant that just laid him off. His wife is, also, out of work, and he has two daughters. We started talking about our faith, and I found out he is, actually, really knowledgeable with the bible and helps out at his church. It's funny how your perception of someone can start to change when you get to know that person a little.

After about ten minutes this pizza of heaping deliciousness

- 126 -

came out, and usually I pray before I eat, but before I got to, Anthony says, "I think we should pray over this food first."

"I was hoping you would say that!" I had the biggest smile on my face.

I put my hand on Anthony's shoulder and said a prayer about how I'm thankful I met him tonight and that I wish the best for him. We both ate a piece and then went our own ways. Before he left he looked at me, and he didn't even have to say anything because I saw in his eyes and smile how pleasantly surprised he was about what just happened.

He could, also, see that I felt the same way.

The difference between right and wrong is a little discomfort. I didn't have to meet Anthony, but I'm glad I did. I learned that not everything is as it seems, and it's so easy to assume. It's so easy to stand on the sidelines and not take a chance. I'm not saying you should strike up a chat with every homeless person and buy them pizza. That would be kind of weird and unnecessary and, possibly, unsafe. What I am saying is, "Give people a chance." Be bold enough to stick a hand out when no one else will. Not only will it be good for that person, I bet you'll like it. That's what leaders do. They do the right thing because it's the right thing to do. They "take" responsibility even if it's not asked or required. They help influence others in a positive way so that they will go on and help themselves.

Think about how Super Leader applies in this story:

- Super Leaders volunteer to be the person to open up and help out,
- Super Leaders think about their actions and don't just react like puppets,

- Super leaders listen more than talk,
- Super leaders maintain a positive attitude,
- Super Leaders have big hearts for people,
- Super Leaders do these things so that they can help light others' ways, AND
- Super Leaders operate with a foundation of character.

So here's an idea: This week, I want you to be confident and say, "What's up?" (something along that line) to someone you don't know very well at your school, church, or wherever. Just get to know them for a few minutes. It will reveal a lot about your character.

Do it now. I'm serious. Just do it!

Courage, not complacency, is our need today.
Leadership not salesmanship.

-John F. Kennedy

KEY POINTS:

- The difference between right and wrong is often a little discomfort, which takes courage.

- You always feel better after doing what's right even if it was hard in the moment.

- You always feel worse after not doing what's right even if it was easy in the moment.

CHAPTER 9

Fight or Flight

It's time. The teacher's voice is getting louder with enthusi-
asm. "This is it!" I stand up from my chair and shake out my arms
and legs. The adrenalin is running full force throughout my body
as I am now jumping up and down like I am getting ready to run
a 200m track race.

It's like that "fight or flight" thing. When life hits you straight in
your face with either an opportunity or a really cruddy situation,
you can either "fight or flight." You can't always choose what
happens, but you can always choose how you respond to what
happens.

Do you fall down and give up or do you dig down and man-up
(or woman-up)?

There is always a choice, and we are always choosing one or
the other whether we know it or not.

You Have More

We have moments in life that change us. These moments are moments of adversity, which reveal our
strengths and uncover our weaknesses. Sometimes
we are forced into adversity, and other times, we choose it
out of pure desire. Sometimes we want something so badly
that we are willing to do almost anything to get it.

I was in seventh grade when I signed up for the cross-country team. I loved sports: basketball, football, and baseball. It's easy to give sweat, blood, and tears when you want it, when you love it. I always dreamed of becoming a professional basketball player and shooting the game-winning shot. The basketball goal in my driveway knew me very well. In snow, sun, and darkness, I was there. I loved basketball.

Although I loved basketball, I was a little out of shape. You see, I had a "chunky" phase when I was a kid. Maybe that was why I never became an exceptional swimmer... because I didn't want to get into the pool since that meant I had to take my shirt off!

Anyway, my basketball coach came up to me one day and said, "Brandon, you need to go out for cross-country." "But wait, coach!" I replied nervously. "Doesn't cross country involve running?" "Yes!" he smiled. "Sometimes, to do what you want to do (play basketball) you have to do what you don't want to do (run)."

I hated cross-country. That entire seventh-grade season was one big embarrassment. I was near last in practices and near last in races—out of over 100 runners! My father always told me, "If you are going to do something, you do it. Never quit in the middle." So, that's what I did. You would think I would have quit after that season of near last finishes, but I didn't, and that made all the difference.

It was the summer before my eighth-grade year, and there was volunteer off-season running for those crazy enough to participate. (I was there.) I ran with a friend of mine, Bryan, who was a lot faster than I was, but being a friend, he slowed down just for me during conditioning. We ran on Main Street, totaling about four miles roundtrip. We would run the usual course at the usual pace, but one day, my friend convinced me to run farther than we had ever run. As we ran he ordered from ahead of me, "Come on, Brandon, you have more than that. Keep going!" I wanted to stop. I wanted to walk so badly. I might have even tried to escape when he wasn't looking. My side felt like grinding forks, and my mouth was one big cotton ball. It was hot and in the middle of summer. I was sweating profusely, and I was NOT having fun. Finally, we came to a stop at the bottom of a big hill in front of McDonald's. What? Jackpot! I'm thinking, "I understand now. We ran a little farther today so that we can eat! And, of course we can just call up one of our moms to pick us up. Brilliant!"

Bryan suddenly turned around and started going back up the hill where we came from. I was struck with confusion and quickly that confusion turned into sheer horror. We weren't done! We were only half way done and now we are going back! Bryan looked over his shoulder and saw me going into shock and said, "Come on, Brandon. You can do it!"

"Umm... no, I can't." I thought.

Even when my conscious told me that there were still miles to go, and there was no way I could make it, I started running again, because I didn't want to let my friend down. He was like, well, a leader to me. Have you ever had a pain in your side when you ran? I don't mean a little tickle in your tummy. I mean a "WHAT IS THAT?!" feeling. Whenever I started slowing down Bryan was there encouraging me. Whenever the "WHAT IS THAT?!" came he pushed me through It. I think we all have a "light" inside that burns when we believe in ourselves, but life can make it go out. Every time my light was going out Bryan would push me and keep it on. Suddenly I realized I was up the hill. That hill looked impossible at the bottom of it... but I did it. You see, that was weird. At that moment something hit me like a light switch flipping on. I realized that when I thought I gave it my all, I had not. I fooled myself. I really did have more, and I could do more than I thought. Like a spark catching flame, my mind took over, and my body became mechanical: legs moving without thought.

That day I finished without stopping! I finished a different person, because I saw myself differently. I used to see myself inside a tiny box, but after that day my box got bigger. And, when you see yourself differently you do things differently, and when you begin to do things differently you continue to see yourself differently. How we see ourselves truly determines what we make of ourselves.

I ran almost every day after that, and before the summer was over... Bryan couldn't keep up with me!

It was my eighth-grade cross-country season, and I was a new *runner; I was a new person.*

My first race.......first place!

My second race......first place!!

My third race......FIRST PLACE!!!!!

And so it went. Friends were shocked by my complete turnaround. My parents were like, "Who are you, and what did you do with our out-of-shape child?!"

I was a superstar in the district. I was "the person to beat." On the day of my final race I was undefeated. Everything was riding on this race. There was energy in the air. New schools with new runners were competing at this race, and one runner in particular, I was told, would be tough to beat.

"Runners, to your mark!" He lifted his gun. Everyone simultaneously crouched in ready position. I knew my undefeated career was riding on this race. Everything I trained for was to be decided in a matter of minutes. "BANG!"

I learned earlier in the season that it is easier to maintain first place than to conserve energy and try to fight to the front later in the race. One minute into the race and I was in first. There were spectators all around cheering, waving arms.

Three minutes into the race... I rounded a corner, and after a hundred feet, a whistle blew, signaling that I was going the wrong way. "YOU GOTTA BE KIDDING ME!" As I turned around all the other runners who were following me also turned around like a wave. Suddenly, I wasn't in the front of the pack anymore... I was in the back of the pack. I was last, and everyone was following me.

The runners next to me looked at what just happened. We saw the same obstacle in front of us, but we look at it differently. You always have two choices in life; give up or work harder. I started running, and as I looked back I saw the others runners walking. Their "light" was out.

100 meters one way means 100 meters back the other way, and 200 meters off course equals an almost ensured loss.

I didn't let it get to me, though. I just knew I had to get to the front of the pack. Each step had purpose. We entered the woods, which were a death trap, and I am not exaggerating. It looked like an off-road hiking trail with rocks, roots, and holes everywhere— the path less than five feet wide.

One by one I passed runners, inching towards the front. A tunnel of light revealed the opening of the woods, and once outside marked the last half mile to the finish line. The light was blinding as I exited the woods, and I could see there was only one runner still ahead of me. It was him; the runner they all said would be hard to beat. As a runner, you have to learn how to conserve your energy and not waste it all at one time. In fact, some schools will have a decoy runner sprint at the beginning just to fool the lead runner into wasting his energy. ...I know, how clever.

I had little time from where I went off course until the last half mile to worry about conserving energy. I pushed myself, and within seconds, we were neck and neck. He was slightly taller than I, blue jersey, short black hair, and I could tell he was saving a sprint for the end. We were a little over a quarter mile from the finish line and still sizing each other up, waiting to see who would sprint first. Our breaths were steady, our strides long. I was tired.

There is something magical about the last 200 meters in a race. It is the last burst of glory, testing what you are really made of. Two rows of spectators lined the path ahead, their shouts and cheers could be heard now, and that is pure runner's fuel floating in the air.

He went for it first, running almost twice as fast, and digging his spikes into the ground with hands pumping hard. It was a one-on-one dead sprint to the end with everything resting on 200 meters of grass and dirt. We were side by side, letting out grunts and pushing for whatever we had left.

It was only a few months since the run on Main Street. I remember the grey concrete sidewalks, my shoes tied tightly, my shirt completely soaked in sweat, and Bryan shouting, "Come on Brandon, you have more than that. Keep going!"

100 feet from the tape, and people were screaming like betters at a race track—two horses running their guts out for the big prize.

I wanted to stop.

I wanted to fall.

My side felt like grinding forks, and my mouth was one big cotton ball. Sweat pourin'... I was not having fun. Even when my body kept telling me, "You can't do it"...I knew better.

60 meters...Keep going. You have more.

50 meters…You have more.

10 meters…YOU HAVE MORE!

30 meters before the finish line—THE FINISH LINE—the other runner gives up. Well, he would probably say that he couldn't do it, but I think he could have. The problem was he didn't think it also. I don't think he was willing to go through the "what is that?!" long enough. You see, we often have to go through what we don't want to do (the pain) to get where we want to go (the success).

With my head and chest lunging forward, I broke the tape— undefeated.

Like a race, every life has a starting line and a finish line. How will you start? How will you finish? Don't be that person who quits 30 meters from the finish line and then tells himself or herself, "I'm just not fast enough." It's a mental race.

So, how did I do that? How did I go from defeated to undefeated in one year? Was it hard work? Yes, but how? Was it believing in myself? Yes, but how?

This story is about me, but I'm not the main character. This story is about a leader. This story is about Bryan. Bryan EMPOWERED me. He helped me realize "I have more." He helped me "build a bigger box" and push through the "WHAT IS THAT?!" If it wasn't for Bryan, I would have never taken on that hill next to McDonald's. Instead, I would have gotten a "Triple Thick Milkshake" (strawberry). I never would have made it to that moment when the light switch flipped on inside of me. Instead, the "light" would have gone out. But it didn't. I went on to become a starter in varsity basketball. I also became STUCO president where I went to a camp and saw a motivational speaker and said, "I want to do that." And, here I am. Oh, and Bryan? He is not a police officer. He's still helping people. Thanks, Bryan.

Leadership is not about being above someone.

Leadership is about being beside someone

...and pushing them above.

What's your "what is that?!" Is your "light" out? How big is your "box"? Take life one step at a time, and no matter how far off course you get, turn around. But remember, we can't do it on our own. We need leadership so that we can become leaders.

"What lies behind us and what lies before us are tiny matters compared to what lies within us."

-Ralph Waldo Emerson

KEY POINTS:

- **Leadership is not about being above someone. Leadership is about being beside someone and pushing them above.**
- **Push through your "What is that?!" and your box will get bigger.**

CHAPTER 10

Let It Move!

I'm walking towards the curtains. "Where's the opening? Dang you black curtains!"

"Why am I here? What is this for?" I remind myself, "To empower others, to make a difference, to help others not be a 'lamesauce'."

With a loud voice, the teacher announces, "Ladies and gentlemen, please put your hands together for..."

I take a deep breath, "I'm ready."

Three People

Think of three people you know and admire. These three people should be "leaders" in your eyes. Now, think of five.

Is it harder? Why? Could it be because "Super Leaders" are becoming harder to find?

Now let me ask you, "Would YOU be on anyone's 'top three' list?"

We need "true" youth leaders who are brave enough to face their fears and live their lives. Now is the time for the young and the bold! When you are faced with a decision to take a stand, go to someone's defense, put your neck on the line, lead, do what's right... When you're faced with that decision, you will get a good feeling deep inside that lets you know, "This is right." When that happens...

LET IT MOVE!

Thank you for reading my book! I'm 100 percent positive that if you think about the things said in this book and apply them this week, you will see a change in your life, and you'll like it. More importantly, though, you will help change other people's lives. Remember, this is not a quick fix thing. Just like anything else (sports, music, math...) it takes practice. Being a leader is a continuous choice. Choose to be a "Super Leader" by listening, thinking, serving, having a positive attitude, having a big heart, helping others find their way, and being grounded in character. You will mess up, but mess-ups are fine as long as you don't give up.

Don't be a Lamesauce. Take a stand and start becoming a better you. You owe it to yourself.

— *Brandon Lee White*

CHAPTER 11

CASE STUDIES

-WWYD?-

This section is designed to provide you with some real-life challenges that you might encounter as a "Super Leader" in your school or organization. You can work on these individually or as a group. The purpose is to get you thinking about practical things student leaders are faced with and to better equip you when responding. So, consider these case studies and think about, as a leader, what would you do?

1. **This is stupid.**
   Have you ever been in a group and there is a project to work on but nobody is involved or cares? There isn't a sense of teamwork or excitement to do anything. Let's look at the following example:
   The student council at "School Awesome" is given the task to plan the school dance. A meeting is held and the STUCO president is 10 minutes late. Meanwhile, a member tries to take the initiative by saying, "Alright guys, we know what we're

supposed to talk about. Let's brainstorm!" Another member replies, "Shut up, you're not the president." Some students laugh while others remain silent. The student who wanted to brainstorm is now disengaged and doesn't care anymore.

The president storms in, "Okay, here we go. We have to plan the school dance. I got it all planned out. We're going to go with my brother's friend who DJs because he's cheap. Oh, and we're gonna get some real fruit punch this year because whatever that punch was last year tasted like vomit. Alright, I gotta go to class."

"Wait!" another member shouts.

"What?" the president responds.

"What are we supposed to do?" the member asks.

"Umm, I don't know. Don't worry about it. "

Another member asks, "What about the decorations?"

"Yeah, figure it out. I gotta go!" The president shouts, while running out the door.

"This sucks." A member responds.

Another member adds, "As long as I don't have to do anything... sounds good to me!"

Questions:

1. Describe what each person individually might feel about the meeting and their STUCO.

2. Describe the lack of teamwork within this group and why it is so bad.

3. What can be done differently by each

member to increase teamwork and a sense
of involvement, starting with the president?

Consider This:
Like a sports team or band, every person has a
specific responsibility. It may be different than
the other person's, but all parts are important.

A student doesn't have to be the STUCO
president to be a leader because he or she can
be a "Super Leader" within his or her specific
responsibility. The student can help the team
succeed by fulfilling his or her own responsibilities and assisting others using the Super Leader's actions: thinking with a level head, having a
positive attitude, listening.

Before anything is done, there needs to be
mutual understanding, mutual involvement, col-
lective opinion gathering, validation of opinions,
and thoughtful consideration of input and feedback. For example, the president should first
state the objective "plan the school dance" and
then encourage everyone to brainstorm and
gather ideas. The more each member feels he
or she has had an input, the more he or she will
want to be involved.

The club needs to hold each other accountable
to their obligations but not yell at them or be
condescending. Build people up, make them

feel involved, give them specific responsibilities that they want to do, compliment them on their progress, and set periodic goals for each task with deadlines to measure progress and to stay on task.

2. Oh, No, She Didn't!

Like any other group, you are probably going to have conflict between members. This is really bad, if not resolved, because it's like a cancer that grows and just kills the effectiveness of the group. However, you will need to attack it in the right way. Let's look at an example:

Jill is a member of student leadership club, and it's her sophomore year. She's really good friends with Kelly, who is a senior and the club president. Meanwhile, Megan is also a member, and she is a junior. She has several friends who are also in the club, including the president, Kelly.

Well, as it usually goes, Megan heard from her friend Stacey that Jill was getting fresh with Megan's boyfriend. Say what?! Umm. So, Megan and Stacey started to make up a bunch of nasty rumors about Jill, posted stuff on Facebook, and blah, blah, blah.

The next meeting rolls around and Jill is the last person to arrive. Megan, Stacey, Kelly, and the other members are already there. Megan quickly whispers something to Stacey, but loud enough that pretty much everyone can hear, and some people start laughing. The president, Kelly, who is also Jill's friend, doesn't say anything.

Jill storms out, mumbling some things under her breath. Another member says, "How are we going to get this assignment done? Jill has most of the research." So the arguing begins with those who are siding with Jill and those who are siding with Stacey. Kelly is remaining out of it and doesn't seem to know what to do. No progress is being made in the meeting, and the club seems to be divided and falling apart.

Questions:
1. Considering all the information, what caused the division in the group?
2. What could have stopped it before it began?
3. Right now, how should the president handle this situation? How should the members handle it? How should Jill handle it?
4. Should there be discipline?
5. How can this be prevented in the future?

Consider This:

Every fire needs fuel to burn. The same is true with conflict. Rumors and cliques are like gasoline to the fire because they fuel the problem, allowing it to get out of control. Like bullying, if bystanders intervene and confront the problem by not allowing cliques to form and walls to go up, the fire can be put out.

Strength in numbers is always a good thing when attacking conflict, but attacking either party should be avoided. Instead, make each person feel understood. This doesn't mean you have to agree with one side or the other by saying, "Oh, I know how you feel! I hate her, too!" Wrong. Instead, focus on helping the group so the outcome is good for both sides.

Talking to Jill or Megan one on one can be good, but going with three or four is also good. Remember, don't say, "You're a jerk! Stop being mean." Instead say something like, "Hey Megan, we know something is going on between you and Jill. We wanted to hear your side of the story. What happened?" Then after she tells you, don't comment on whether you agree or disagree. Instead, you might say something like, "We understand you're really upset with all of this and, like you, we don't want our STUCO falling apart. Let's just find a way to make things okay." Eventually, you will probably want to get both of them together to talk, but in due time, or they might cause serious damage to each other.

The president is not the only person who has the responsibility to make sure the group is healthy. It's everyone's responsibility. If you are not actively working every day to maintain a healthy relationship with the entire group, you are not a "Super Leader." I'm not saying you have to be best friends with everyone, but you do have to treat everyone with respect and do what's right.

3. Who Cares?!

Getting people involved and excited about a project can be hard. Whether it's in your club or outside of the club, like the entire school, it's difficult getting everyone "fired up" about what you're doing. Without enthusiasm, you don't have much involvement. Without involvement, you don't have good results. Here's an example:

"The Awesomesauce Club" was planning a fundraiser to raise awareness and money for a specific cause. They planned it out, but when the day of the event came, the turnout was, well, embarrassing. They didn't understand. They put some fliers up and made announcements, but still, hardly anyone showed up. They were discouraged because of the time they put into it and because they felt no one cared. As a result, the attitude of the club went down, and no one wanted to do anymore fundraisers.

Questions:
1. What are some possible reasons why no one showed up?
2. What are some possible solutions on what they could have done differently?

3. What can be done now to get the club going again and to ensure it keeps positive morale?

Consider This:

Whenever you're planning an event, you need to remember what everyone asks themselves before doing something: What's In It For Me? (WIIFM). Yeah, I know it sounds selfish, but there's a lot of truth in it. Give your "good cause" wings with extra reasons on why they should come.   Entertainment, prizes, extra credit, and competitive games are some ways to "spice" up your event. Another way is incorporating other groups into the event. For example, maybe it's a "guys vs. girls" thing or maybe it's something like a talent show where other clubs are competing against each other. If you make others part of your event, you tap into their contacts. BOOYAH! Part of getting morale back is by understanding what went wrong. Gathering feedback from members and outsiders who didn't go to the event helps everyone under-stand how to improve. Once there is more of an understanding and a better plan, confidence starts coming back.

Before putting on an event, ask outsiders if they would go to it, and why or why not. Ask them to be completely honest so you get valid answers. This will help prevent a lot of frustration.

ABOUT THE AUTHOR

Author, speaker, and youth mover, Brandon Lee White has spoken to thousands of youth through student conferences, school assemblies, leadership events, graduations, camps, and more. He has been featured on TLC, Discovery Health, and FitTV. His purpose is to help youth take ownership of who they are, what they want, and what holds them back in leadership and life.

Brandon is also a professional ballroom dance instructor. In 2009, Brandon founded "Step In Step Out!" - a youth ballroom dance program centered on personal growth and physical fitness.

Brandon attended Rockhurst University where he earned his Master's in Business as well as a double major in Business and Psychology. Brandon encourages youth to seek higher education in what they love to do.

In his spare time Brandon enjoys sports, hunting/fishing, reading the bible, barbecuing, and meeting awesome people as he travels the country. He currently lives in Kansas City, Missouri, where he and his wife, Rachel, help lead the youth group at their church.

LINKS·

Website: www.brandonleewhite.com
Email: Brandon@brandonleewhite.com
Facebook: www.facebook.com/youthmover
Twitter: www.twitter.com/youthmover
Instagram: Youthmover
YouTube: www.youtube.com/whiteble